BENEATH THE CROSS

The Stories of Those Who Stood at the Cross of Jesus

THE MORNING OF THE RESURRECTION, Edward Burne-Jones (1822-1898). © Christie's Images/SuperStock (866-3583).

BENEATH THE CROSS OF JESUS
ELIZABETH C. CLEPHANE

Beneath the cross of Jesus
I fain would take my stand,
The shadow of a mighty rock
Within a weary land;
A home within the wilderness,
A rest upon the way,
From the burning of the noontide heat,
And the burden of the day.

Upon the cross of Jesus
Mine eye at times can see
The very dying form of one
Who suffered there for me;

And from my smitten heart with tears
Two wonders I confess—
The wonders of his glorious love
And my unworthiness.

I take, O cross, thy shadow
For my abiding place;
I ask no other sunshine than
The sunshine of his face;
Content to let the world go by,
To know no gain nor loss,
My sinful self my only shame,
My glory all the cross. Amen.

Beneath the Cross

The Stories of Those Who Stood at the Cross of Jesus

Patricia A. Pingry and Julie K. Hogan, Editors

IDEALS PUBLICATIONS
NASHVILLE, TENNESSEE

ISBN 0-8249-5857-8

Published by Ideals Publications
A division of Guideposts
535 Metroplex Drive, Suite 250
Nashville, Tennessee 37211
www.idealsbooks.com

Printed and bound in U.S.A. by RR Donnelley, Willard, Ohio

Color separations by Precision Color Graphics, Franklin, Wisconsin

Library of Congress CIP data on file

Front cover painting: THE EARTHQUAKE. James J. Tissot (1826–1902). © SuperStock (999-50).

10 9 8 7 6 5 4 3 2 1

Publisher, Patricia A. Pingry
Art Director, Eve DeGrie
Copy Editor, Melinda Rathjen
Permissions Editor, Patsy Jay

Book Design by Eve DeGrie

Display type is Memento Mori by Red Eye Type
Text type is Galliard
Captions and Scripture type is Futura

ACKNOWLEDGMENTS

BARCLAY, William. "John" from *The Master's Men*. Copyright © 1959 by William Barclay. Published by SCM Press Ltd. BATTLE, Gerald N. "John" from *Armed with Love*. Copyright © 1973 by Abingdon Press. BISHOP, Jim. "The Watch Is Set," "A Shining Triumph," "An Act of Courage," and "Loving Kindness for the Messiah" from *The Day Christ Died* by Jim Bishop. Copyright © 1957, 1977. Published by HarperCollins. BORDEN, Mary. "Love Stood at a Distance" and "The Deposition" from *The King of the Jews* by Mary Borden. Published by Little, Brown & Company. Used by permission of Duff Hart-Davis. CALDWELL, Taylor. "I, Judas" from *I, Judas* by Taylor Caldwell and Jesse Stearn. Copyright © 1977 by the authors. Published by Atheneum, NY. COSTAIN, Thomas B. "The Silver Chalice" from *The Silver Chalice*. Copyyright © 1952 by Thomas B. Costain. published by Doubleday & Company. DOUGLAS, Lloyd C. "The Big Fisherman" from *The Big Fisherman*. Copyright © 1948 by Lloyd C. Douglas. Published by Houghton Mifflin Company. Used by permission of the Estate of Lloyd C. Douglas. "From the Sixth to the Ninth Hour" and "And They Cast Lots" from *The Robe* by Lloyd C. Douglas. Copyright © 1942 by the author and renewed 1969 by Virginia Douglas Dawson and Betty Douglas Wilson. Reprinted by permission of Houghton Mifflin Company. HOYER, Robert. "The Voice of Caiaphas" and "Peter and John" from *I Remember the Savior's Death*. Copyright © 1955 by Northwestern Publishing House, Milwaukee. KAGAWA, Toyohiko. "The Empty Tomb" from *Behold the Man* by Toyohiko Kagawa. Copyright © 1941 by Harper & Bros. KENNEDY, Pamela. "The Other Woman at the Tomb," "Mary of Magdala," "God's Friday," "The Power to Change," "The Centurion's Story," "Guard Duty," "John," "Simon Peter, the Rock," "Joseph of Arimathea" and "Simon of Cyrene." Copyright © by Pamela Kennedy. Used by permission. KORTRAY, Walter A. "Malchus the Wounded Enemy" from *People Around Jesus* by Walter A. Kortray. Copyright © 1974 by United Church Press. Used by permission of The Pilgrim Press. LAGERKVIST, Par. "Barabbas" from *Barabbas* by Par Lagerkvist, translated by Alan Blair. Copyright © 1951 by Random House, Inc. and renewed 1979 by Pierry Maury, Alan Blair and Katherine Gide. Used by permission of Random House. LEAVELL, Landrum P. "Peter" from *Twelve Who Followed Jesus*. Copyright © 1975 by Broadman & Holman, subsequently assigned to the author. Used by permission of the author. MILLS, James R. "Memoirs of Pontius Pilate" from *Memoirs of Pontius Pilate* by James R. Mills. Copyright © 2000 by Fleming H. Revell. Used by permission of Baker Book House. MURPHY, Edward R. "The Scarlet Lily" from *The Scarlet Lily* by Edward R. Murphy. Copyright © 1944 by Bruce Publishing Co. OURSLER, Fulton. "The Repentant Thief" from *The Greatest Story Ever Told*. Copyright © 1949 by Fulton Oursler. Used by permission of Doubleday, a division of Random House, Inc. POTEAT, Edwin McNeill. "The Faith of the Centurion" from *These Shared His Cross* by Edwin McNeill Poteat. Published by Harper Brothers, 1941. ROLAND, Nicholas. "Who Came by Night" from *Who Came by Night* by Nicholas Roland. Copyright © 1971. Published by Holt, Rinehart and Winston. WALSH, John Evangelist. "The Women at the Tomb" and "Joanna and Salome" from *The Man Who Buried Jesus* by John Evangelist Walsh. Copyright © 1989 by the author. Published by Collier Books, Macmillan, 1989. WATSON, Elizabeth G. "Mary, the Wife of Clopas, Remembers" from *Wisdom Daughters: Stories of Women Around Jesus* by Elizabeth G. Watson. Copyright © 1997 by the author. Used by permission of The Pilgrim Press.

Every effort has been made to contact the copyright owners of each selection printed in this book. Should errors be found, please contact the publisher.

CONTENTS

THE BEGINNING AND THE END

ACCORDING TO THE GOSPELS OF MATTHEW AND LUKE

And in the sixth month the angel Gabriel was sent from God unto a city of Galilee, named Nazareth, to a virgin espoused to a man whose name was Joseph, of the house of David; and the virgin's name was Mary.

And the angel said unto her, Fear not, Mary: for thou hast found favour with God. And, behold, thou shalt conceive in thy womb, and bring forth a son, and shalt call his name JESUS. He shall be great, and shall be called the Son of the Highest: and the Lord God shall give unto him the throne of his father David: And he shall reign over the house of Jacob for ever; and of his kingdom there shall be no end.

And Mary said, My soul doth magnify the Lord, And my spirit hath rejoiced in God my Saviour. For he hath regarded the low estate of his handmaiden: for, behold, from henceforth all generations shall call me blessed. For he that is mighty hath done to me great things; and holy is his name (Luke 1:26–27, 30–33, 46-49).

But while he [Joseph] thought on these things, behold, the angel of the Lord appeared unto him in a dream, saying, Joseph, thou son of David, fear not to take unto thee Mary thy wife: for that which is conceived in her is of the Holy Ghost. And she shall bring forth a son, and thou shalt call his name JESUS: for he shall save his people from their sins. (Matthew 1:20–21).

And there were in the same country shep-herds abiding in the field, keeping watch over their flock by night. And, lo, the angel of the Lord came upon them, and the glory of the Lord shone round about them: and they were sore afraid. And the angel said unto them, Fear not: for, behold, I bring you good tidings of great joy, which shall be to all people. For unto you is born this day in the city of David a Saviour, which is Christ the Lord. And this shall be a sign unto you; Ye shall find the babe wrapped in swaddling clothes, lying in a manger. And suddenly there was with the angel a multitude of the heavenly host praising God, and saying, Glory to God in the highest, and on earth peace, good will toward men.

And it came to pass, as the angels were gone away from them into heaven, the shep-herds said one to another, Let us now go even unto Bethlehem, and see this thing which is come to pass, which the Lord hath made known unto us. And they came with haste, and found Mary, and Joseph, and the babe lying in a manger. And when they had seen it, they made known abroad the saying which was told them concerning this child. And all they that heard it wondered at those things which were told them by the shepherds. But Mary kept all these things, and pondered them in her heart (Luke 2:8-19).

Now when Jesus was born in Bethlehem of Judaea in the days of Herod the king, behold, there came wise men from the east to Jerusalem . . . When they had heard the king, they departed; and, lo, the star, which they saw in the east, went before them, till it came and stood over where the young child was. . . . And when they were come into the house, they saw the young child with Mary his mother, and fell down, and worshipped him: and when they had opened their treasures, they presented unto him gifts; gold, and frankincense, and myrrh (Matthew 2:1, 9, 11).

THIRTY-THREE YEARS LATER . . .

And they crucified him, and parted his garments, casting lots: that it might be fulfilled which was spoken by the prophet, They parted my garments among them, and upon my vesture did they cast lots. And sitting down they watched him there; And set up over his head his accusation written, THIS IS JESUS THE KING OF THE JEWS.

Then were there two thieves crucified with him, one on the right hand, and another on the left. And they that passed by reviled him, wagging their heads, And saying, Thou that destroyest the temple, and buildest it in three days, save thyself. If thou be the Son of God, come down from the cross.

Likewise also the chief priests mocking him, with the scribes and elders, said, He saved others; himself he cannot save. If he be the King of Israel, let him now come down from the cross, and we will believe him. He trusted in God; let him deliver him now, if he will have him: for he said, I am the Son of God. . . .

Now from the sixth hour there was darkness over all the land unto the ninth hour. And about the ninth hour Jesus cried with a loud voice, saying, *Eli, Eli, lama sabachthani?* that is to say, My God, my God, why hast thou forsaken me? Some of them that stood there, when they heard that, said, This man calleth for Elias. And straightway one of them ran, and took a sponge, and filled it with vinegar, and put it on a reed, and gave him to drink. The rest said, Let be, let us see whether Elias will come to save him.

Jesus, when he had cried again with a loud voice, yielded up the ghost. And, behold, the veil of the temple was rent in twain from the top to the bottom; and the earth did quake, and the rocks rent; And the graves were opened; and many bodies of the saints which slept arose, And came out of the graves after his resurrection, and went into the holy city, and appeared unto many. Now when the centurion, and they that were with him, watching Jesus, saw the earthquake, and those things that were done, they feared greatly, saying, Truly this was the Son of God (Matthew 27:35–43, 45–54).

BENEATH THE CROSS

THE WOMEN

There were also women looking on afar off: among whom was Mary Magdalene, and Mary the mother of James the less and of Joses, and Salome; (Who also, when he was in Galilee, followed him, and ministered unto him;) and many other women which came up with him unto Jerusalem. . . . And Mary Magdalene and Mary the mother of Joses beheld where he was laid. And when the sabbath was past, Mary Magdalene, and Mary the mother of James, and Salome, had bought sweet spices, that they might come and anoint him. And very early in the morning the first day of the week, they came unto the sepulchre at the rising of the sun (MARK 15:40–41; 16:1–2).

MATER DOLOROSA, James J. Tissot (1836–1902).
© SuperStock (999-431).

MARY
THE MOTHER OF JESUS
GOD'S FRIDAY

PAM KENNEDY

Mary sighed and leaned her head back against the rough wall of her house. When the two distraught disciples had come rapping at her door with the news that Jesus had been arrested and taken to the high priest, she had wrapped herself in her shawl, suddenly chilled. After their departure, she sank down upon a small wooden bench near the doorway. Jesus had built the bench years ago when he was just a boy in Joseph's carpenter shop. She ran her fingers along its smooth edges, smiling slightly as she recalled his pride when he had presented it to her. So many memories tumbled through her mind. She raised her eyes and watched the myriad stars shimmering in the black sky. They seemed to be spinning, spiraling in the darkness, drawing her upward, upward and back in time to another night, long ago. . . .

So many nights, some filled with wonder, others with pain, had passed since then. She closed her eyes and sighed once more. What would this night bring? She did not fear the darkness, for she had learned long ago that God is light and in him is no darkness. But she also knew that men preferred their own darkness to God's light. Where was her son now? Into what darkness had they taken him? She remembered the song she sang long ago as she shared Gabriel's news with Elizabeth.

"My soul glorifies the Lord and my spirit rejoices in God my Savior, for he has been mindful of the humble state of his servant. From now on all generations will call me blessed, for the Mighty One has done great things for me—holy is his name" (Luke 1:46–49 NIV).

She opened her eyes and looked into the vastness of the night. The Lord's greatness and blessings were both precious and painful, yet she would not have traded a moment of her life for that of another. And now, the Lord was asking her to walk with him along a new path. As if reaching out in obedience once again, she lifted her hand toward the heavens and whispered, "I am the Lord's servant."

She sat thus, as still as a statue, until the pale shimmer of dawn crept over the hilltops and pushed its way slowly into her awareness. In the shadowed street she glimpsed a woman hurrying toward her.

Now there stood by the cross of Jesus his mother (JOHN 19:25).

CRUCIFIXION, Titan (1477/89–1576), HERMITAGE MUSEUM, SAINT PETERSBURG, RUSSIA,
© HERMITAGE MUSEUM, ST. PETERSBURG, RUSSIA/SUPERSTOCK (261-572)

"Mary!" the woman called, and Mary recognized the voice of her sister. Standing, she received the wife of Clopas with a warm embrace. "They've taken Jesus and held a mockery of a trial," her sister gasped between breaths. She wrung her hands and continued, "Even now they are dragging him before Pilate, begging for his crucifixion! Do you think we should go to him?"

Mary stiffened as if pierced with a sword and grasped the other woman's hand. "We will remain here and pray. The Lord will tell us what we should do. Come, dear sister." They went inside and knelt together on the hard floor.

Hours later, they were still there when the Apostle John came to the house with the dreadful news. The time had come. Quickly they

pulled their shawls over their heads and hurried with him to Golgotha.

Mary stood in the midst of the crowd, yet felt alone, staring at her oldest son. She recalled his first steps, his first words, and the way he ran to show her the precise symmetry of a butterfly's wing or the smooth-grained beauty of a well-made table. Her love silently reached out to him above the din of the shouting crowd, and he slowly turned his head as if in response to the cry of her heart. She raised her arms toward him and caught his eyes with her own. It was as if her grieving soul calmed in that moment. Time stopped, and all the fragments of the past thirty-three years fell into place: the Annunciation, the prophetic words of Anna and Simeon, the escape and return from Egypt, the words Jesus spoke in the Temple when he was only twelve, his teaching and miracles, his prayers and healings. These and thousands of other words and images suddenly coincided in an eternal tapestry, and Mary realized the truth. This execution on a barren Judean hillside was not just an evil perpetrated by mere men. In that moment Mary saw the fulfillment of God's perfect plan. Through the sacrifice of Christ's death would come the long-promised hope of everlasting life. When she had spoken her own words of obedience as a girl, she had not known all that they would mean. But when she heard Jesus say, "Father, into your hands I commend my spirit," she understood the price of commitment.

When the terrible darkness of the afternoon lifted and the figures on the three crosses were still, Mary allowed the Apostle John to lead her gently down the hillside to her home. She assured him she would be fine and urged him to go comfort the others. That night, she sat again on the bench that Jesus had made as a boy, looking out at the shimmering stars, knowing what the others would soon discover. This day was not an ending but a beginning. She leaned back against the wall of the house and closed her eyes. Her fingers slowly traced the straight, smooth edge of the bench her son had made, and she smiled as she drifted into sleep.

CALVARY by Andrea Mantegna (1431–1506) Musee de Louvre, Paris, France. © Musee de Louvre, Paris/SuperStock (1158-2205).

THE SCARLET LILY

EDWARD F. MURPHY

The mother's cheek, whiter than the asphodels of Nazareth, touched the holy tree. A warm breeze, redolent of gardens, penetrated the icy air. Mary Magdalene was reminded of a little grave in Galilee, alive with flowers, where the child Samuel, who had breathed his last in Jesus' arms, lay; and she prayed that the Lord himself might now rest in the embrace of his Father.

A rift through the clouds made a deep cleft in the sky. The last door had opened. "Father," throbbed his voice, as meager as that of a tired child, and then suddenly loud with longing, "into your hands, I commend my spirit."

Mary raised her tear-stained face in the light. At last her understanding was complete. The evidence seemed as clear as the waters of Cana which had once reddened into wine; she blushed that it had taken her so long to see the truth. His kingdom was not greatness but goodness; not exterior pomp but interior perfection; not the restoration of an earthly Israel but the foundation of a spiritual one. Earth had experi-enced and would experience its Herods—proud, selfish, cruel, decadent—and multitudes had writhed and would writhe under their sway; but here was the only kind of king that could rule hearts, and with his very wounds heal them. She had once believed that his birth brought death, but now knew that his death meant life—the only life worth living—the life of the spirit. And the living spirit was love.

Her mind reverted over the long stretch of years to the hillside of Bethlehem where shepherds still watched their flocks, angels had linked two worlds, and a child had been born. "He will be reborn over and over again," she told herself, "in the lives of the lowly, the con-trite, the humble."

Another thought brought the balm of Gilead to her soul: on the night of his nativity, a star had shone down from heaven to earth; and now, in the day of his deliverance, his perfect sacrifice, starlike, was shin-ing up from earth to heaven.

Holding the hand of his mother, she rubbed her eyes. The unutterable horror of Calvary had burned away like a mist,

> There were also women looking on afar off: among whom was Mary Magda-lene, and Mary the mother of James the less and of Joses, and Salome; (Who also, when he was in Galilee, followed him, and ministered unto him;) and many other women which came up with him unto Jerusalem (MARK 15:40–41).

SCARLET DAYLILY, © Ping Amranand/SuperStock (182-2938E)

even as all blood had drained from the body that hung glimmering on the cross.

The king had entered his kingdom.

Two lilies—the one white, the other scarlet; the one straight in the sun, the other bending its head but curling its petals upward—reared their beauty in the wake of his glory, a pledge of an undying spring.

MARY, HIS MOTHER

SHOLEM ASCH

Miriam was a woman in her early fifties when she came to Jerusalem. Throughout her years with Yeshua in Nazareth, God in his mercy had preserved her beauty and the freshness of her youth. During this last year, since her son's going forth, age had struck her without warning. It was a heavy-laden [Miriam] that Jochanan led through the streets of the city.

The day was Thursday, before the eve of the Passover. Miriam carried a small bundle of things she was bringing her son—the cloak without seams she had been weaving these past months and a cruse of clear oil for his hair; and, in a gourd bottle tied to the bundle, wine for the consecration of the feast.

The narrow streets were dense with pilgrims and Jochanan had to jostle for every inch of passage. . . . To Miriam, struggling behind Jochanan through the crowds, it seemed that this vast confluence of pilgrims had gathered here for the sake of her son. She thought the people knew what great events were pending on this feast day in the Holy City, as though angelic heralds had roused them from their homes to hasten to Jerusalem and become witnesses of her son's glory. . . .

The congestion of the pilgrims, the ceaseless tumult, and the agitation caused by armed soldiers in the crowd—all this, Miriam felt, must have a bearing on her son, and the thought made her heart beat faster.

It was in a high state of excitement that she finally reached the house of Joanna, the wife of the Herodian official, where the women who had come with Yeshua from Galilee were staying. [Miriam's] sister Mariama, Shoshannah, Zebedee's widow, and several other women were waiting to welcome her. Mariama, upon seeing her, burst into tears and began to kiss her hands. The others roused and bestirred themselves to wash her feet and offer her food. Miriam thanked them but declined to eat; she was too anxious to hear about her son—where he resided and how he had fared in Jerusalem.

Mariama began to answer her questions. She said that Yeshua and his disciples spent their days in the Temple, where Yeshua preached to the people and apprised them of his mis-

> Is not this the carpenter's son? is not his mother called Mary? and his brethren, James, and Joses, and Simon, and Judas? And his sisters, are they not all with us? Whence then hath this man all these things (MATTHEW 13:55–56)?

sion. Great numbers, she said, gathered about him to drink up his message, cherishing his every word as sheer gospel.

Then the other women joined in the telling, and the mother heard how Yeshua had entered Jerusalem riding an ass richly caparisoned, and how the people had hailed him with branches and wreaths and cries of "Hosanna" and "Son of David." They related how he had cast out all those who sold and bought in the Temple and had publicly rebuked the learned and the Sadducees and the officers of the priesthood. They told that he had said that he could destroy the Temple and build it up again within three days, for which blasphemy the officers of the Temple sought to arrest him and bring him to trial, but would not, for fear of the populace which thronged about him as soon as he appeared within its courts.

It was manifest from the description of the women that the day of her son's glory was approaching at last. It could be tomorrow, or the following day, and Yeshua was making ready. He was taking leave of his disciples and preparing to depart; and he had warned them that they too would drink of his cup.

For the first time Miriam now saw the woman of whom she had heard so much, the woman Yeshua had cleansed of seven devils, who had repented of her former life and joined the womenfolk who served the rabbi. They called her Miriam of Magdala. Miriam was told that once, in the leper's house, the Magdalene

had opened a teasured alabaster box of ointment to anoint the master's feet. One of the disciples had chided her a wastrel, seeing that the precious spikenard might have been sold for three hundred pence and the money given to the poor. But the master had upheld her, saying: "Let her alone; against the day of my burial has she anointed me."

Miriam listened silently. But at the word "burial" she winced as though a knife had been sunk into her heart.

STREET IN JERUSALEM. © Zefa/H. Armstrong Roberts (KR-18541-gT).

MARY, THE MOTHER OF JESUS

Then returned they unto Jerusalem from the mount called Olivet, which is from Jerusalem a sabbath day's journey. And when they were come in, they went up into an upper room, where abode . . . These all continued with one accord in prayer and supplication, with the women, and Mary the mother of Jesus . . . .And when the day of Pentecost was fully come, they were all with one accord in one place. And suddenly there came a sound from heaven as of a rushing mighty wind, and it filled all the house where they were sitting. And there appeared unto them cloven tongues like as of fire, and it sat upon each of them (ACTS 1:12–14; 2:1–3).

Most of the women who stood at the cross of Jesus had followed him throughout his ministry. They had seen the miracles he performed, they mourned his death, and they rejoiced at his Resurrection. But with Jesus, the Christ, the Resurrection was not the end of the story. After Christ's Resurrection, he walked the earth forty days and nights, eating with his disciples and appearing to many. It is very possible that he also visited with his mother during this time. Mary may have been at his Ascension into heaven.

We don't know these details, but the writer of the Book of Acts does tell us that "the women, and Mary the mother of Jesus" were at the founding of the Christian church. After the Ascension of Christ into heaven, his disciples, the women, and his mother returned to Jerusalem. There, in an upper room they gathered together and waited for the coming of the Holy Spirit, the comforter that Jesus promised to send to his followers. This is the last mention in the Bible of Mary, the mother of Jesus.

Although the Bible doesn't tell us what happens to Mary, the mother of Jesus, we know that her son provided for her earthly comfort through the Apostle John and that she was one of the very first Christians. Mary, the mother of Christ, remains through the ages an example to all for her faith and her obedience to God.

VIRGIN OF THE ANNUNCIATION, Bartolome Estban Murillo. © Superstock.

MARY
THE WIFE OF CLOPAS

THE OTHER MARY REMEMBERS

ELIZABETH G. WATSON

Now it was all over. No miracle had saved Jesus at the last minute. We women had joined the great curious crowd steaming toward Golgotha, "the place of the skull." I went up close to where the crosses were being prepared and joined his mother and her sister. Soon Mary Magdalene came to be with us also. As I sat there now on this first day of the week, waiting for Clopas, I wept as I remembered.

Clopas startled me by touching my shoulder. I stood up and leaned against him, still weeping. After a moment I asked him what had taken so long. He said the men had told him that Mary Magdalene had gone to the tomb early this very morning and found the stone rolled away and the tomb empty. Later she said she had seen Jesus alive and that he had asked her to deliver a message to them. The men did not believe her story. It seemed like an idle tale from an overwrought woman.

We walked as we talked and soon reached the Damascus Gate. We paused to look back over the city. Clopas spoke aloud the

> And many women were there beholding afar off, which followed Jesus from Galilee, ministering unto him: Among which was Mary Magdalene, and Mary the mother of James and Joses, and the mother of Zebedee's children
> MATTHEW 27:55–56)

words that we both remembered hearing Jesus say: "O Jerusalem, Jerusalem, thou that killest the prophets, and stonest them which are sent unto thee, how often would I have gathered thy children together, even as a hen gathereth her chickens under her wings, and ye would not" (Matthew 23:37).

Now we turned our faces homeward on the road to Emmaus. We would have to hurry to make it home before dark. It had been warm during the day, but now a chill wind came up. We pulled the hoods of our cloaks over our heads and held them tightly so they would not blow off.

Walking became difficult. The wind seemed to push us back toward the city. I linked my free arm in Clopas's to steady myself. We were both very tired, and we began to argue. Clopas was sure the men were right, that Jesus could not be alive. He said, "You yourself saw him die." And yet I knew without doubt that Mary Magdalene would not make up such a story. I wanted to believe that she had really seen Jesus.

The road had seemed deserted, and yet presently there was another traveler going in our direction. His hood was pulled over his head and we could not see him clearly. I hoped that he would simply pass us and move on. I did not want to make small talk with a stranger. I felt upset that he continued to walk beside us.

Presently he said, "What were you two talking about?" Clopas stopped and blurted out, "Are you the only person in Jerusalem who does not know what has happened?" And the stranger asked, "What happened?" Clopas told him we were talking about Jesus of Nazareth, a. great prophet, who had been crucified. He went on to say that some of the women among his followers had found the tomb empty this very morning and were sure that he had risen from the dead, but the men, of course, did not believe their story.

The stranger said that it sounded as if what had happened fulfilled the ancient prophecies. He began quoting passages from the books of Moses and also from the Psalms and the Prophets, explaining what they meant as he talked. Our companion was obviously a rabbi. He quoted the prophet Isaiah: "He is despised and rejected of men; a man of sorrows, and acquainted with grief . . . Surely he hath borne our griefs, and carried our sorrows (Isaiah 53:3a, 4a).

"Yes," I said, "that is how it was." Clopas nudged me. It was not proper for a woman to speak to a man she did not know. I had forgotten myself. Jesus always wanted to know what I thought. Clopas would give his opinion on something, and Jesus would say, "But what do you think, Mary?"

Our companion went on with passage after passage. Then I felt that he was speaking directly to me: "Rejoice greatly, O daughter Zion! Shout aloud, O daughter Jerusalem! Lo, your king comes to you; triumphant and victorious is he, humble and riding on a donkey . . . he shall command peace to the nations" (Zechariah 9:9, 10b).

I remembered Jesus riding into Jerusalem on a donkey on the day of the Passover. I thought of Mary Magdalene again, and now I somehow felt sure that what she said was true. Jesus was alive, again!

Clopas stopped suddenly. We were at Emmaus. We were already at the door of our house. We had been so tired and depressed. Walking had seemed such an effort, but listening to this rabbi had made the miles fly by quickly.

The stranger raised his hand in farewell and started to move on. Clopas said, "Stay with us. The day is far spent." He nodded and we walked into the empty house. Clopas groped for the lamp and I went to the garden in the fading light and found a few vegetables. I could always make unleavened bread. I found a bit of dried fish in the cupboard to add to the vegetables.

While I busied myself with this simple

meal, Clopas brought water and washed the feet of our guest. The lamp was dim and flickering. The rabbi was sitting in a dark corner of the room and Clopas could not see his feet clearly.

When the meal was ready the men went to the table. I carried the unleavened bread and set it before our learned guest so that he could bless and break it. Tears ran down as I remembered carrying the bread to Jesus at the Passover meal, just three nights before. I wiped my tears with the back of my hand and watched the rabbi take the bread.

Suddenly I knew those hands, those graceful gestures. Then I saw the wounds in the hands. The lamp which had been flickering flared up and illuminated his face. It was Jesus! He called us both by name. And then he was gone. He did not rise and go out the door, he simply was no longer there. Perhaps you think this an old woman's tale, but Clopas experienced it too. We stood there amazed. Finally Clopas said, "Did not our hearts burn within us while he talked to us on the road?"

I nodded. "Rejoice greatly!" I said.

How could we eat our meal and go to bed as if this were an ordinary homecoming? I put the food away and Clopas extinguished the lamp. We set out in the darkness for Jerusalem, half running in our eagerness.

We found the men still gathered in the upper room. They greeted us with excitement. Peter had also seen Jesus, and everyone acknowledged now that Mary Magdalene had been right. We told them what had happened to us on the road to Emmaus, and how we had known him in the breaking of the bread.

Even as we finished our story, there he was again, in the midst of us, in the familiar room. We all saw him. Some were startled and afraid, remembering how they had hidden in fear while he went to his death. Jesus spoke reassuringly to them. One of the women brought in unleavened bread. He blessed and broke it and passed it to us, saying, "Remember me when you break your bread." And then, once again, he was gone.

In the years since then people have questioned whether his body rose from the dead and was truly with us, or whether it was his spirit that we experienced. Some believe one, and some the other. But I say to you, it does not matter. Love is stronger than death, and those who love are not separated by death. They live on in one another.

UPPER ROOM IN JERUSALEM, SITE OF THE LAST SUPPER.
© R.Opfer/H. Armstrong Roberts, (KR–63539).

STABAT MATER (WOMAN BEHOLD THY SON), James J. Tissot (1836–1902). © Superstock (999-300).

MARY, THE WIFE OF CLOPAS

There were also women looking on afar off: among whom was Mary Magdalene, and Mary the mother of James the less and of Joses, and Salome; (Who also, when he was in Galilee, followed him, and ministered unto him;) and many other women which came up with him unto Jerusalem. He [Pilate] gave the body to Joseph. And he bought fine linen, and took him down, and wrapped him in the linen, and laid him in a sepulchre which was hewn out of a rock, and rolled a stone unto the door of the sepulchre. And Mary Magdalene and Mary the mother of Joses beheld where he was laid. And when the sabbath was past, Mary Magdalene, and Mary the mother of James, and Salome, had bought sweet spices, that they might come and anoint him (MARK 15:40–41, 45–47, 16:1).

According to tradition, Mary was the wife of Clopas (Cleophas in the KJV), who was also called Alphaeus and the mother of the disciple James and Joses. (In contrast to the preceding fictional story, scholars agree that Clopas [Alphaeus] was not the same person as Cleopas who met Christ on the road to Emmaus.)

Most scholars believe that Mary was part of a group of women who followed Jesus and his disciples and provided food and financial assistance for them. Her loyalty to the Master placed her at the crucifixion with Mary, Jesus' mother, and Mark tells us that she was at the burial of Jesus. Her faithfulness was rewarded when she, "the other Mary" went to the tomb on the third day to anoint the body with spices and she discovered that Jesus was still alive.

MARY MAGDALENE
THE DEPOSITION

Mary Borden

Her master was dead. But she could not think that it was so. She had watched him die, had heard his last loud cry of agony, had seen his head drop on his breast. But her mind, her heart, her soul refused to acknowledge what she had seen and heard. She was a strong woman, a woman of the soil of Galilee, passionate, primitive, fearless and reckless under excitement. Her chest was deep, her shoulders were broad, her thighs were sinewed as a man's. And she had been, so men said, possessed of seven devils in the days when she was a dancer. Now she was possessed by love for the man who had saved her and lifted her into heaven. What did she care for the sight of her eyes and the knowledge of her brain? Let her eyes drop out of their sockets; let her brain crack in its skull, she knew that he could not die.

The light shone on him now. A flickering light played over his body. It bathed his feet that were nailed together; it licked at his side, where someone had plunged a spear; it touched his helpless hands that were stretched palms outward with a nail through each palm. And as the torches flared higher, it shone up into his face and, by some trick of the wind that eddied down into the gully, it seemed to make him smile. But he did not lift his head or look up to see what they were doing to him. Even when one of the soldiers climbed up the cross and began to undo the thongs that bound him, he made no sign of any kind.

The other Mary whispered: "They are going to take him down. Please God, they are going to bury him. Look, it is the centurion who was here before, the one who bowed his head when he was dying," and she plucked at the other's sleeve. But Mary Magdalene held her at arm's length and seemed not to hear what she said. Her eyes were starting out of their sockets and her breath came hissing between her lips like the hiss of a snake. They were drawing the nails from his hands and feet, and the soldier who was astride the top of the cross was about to tear the hand loose, for the nail was driven deep into the wood. Why not? Why should he handle the flesh of a dead criminal with care? Mary Magdalene crouched like an animal about to spring.

But the centurion called in time, "Have a care. Go quietly, there, with those hands."

And the soldier, though he gaped stupidly from his perch, did as he was told, drawing the nail out carefully enough, as such things go.

They had loosed all the ropes that bound

him by this time; and once the hands were free, the body slid sideways suddenly and, though the Roman grasped it quickly from above by the arms, it almost slipped from his grasp. But at last it was done. He was lifted down, and the soldiers laid him on the stretcher, where Joseph of Arimathaea and Nicodemus had spread a linen cloth.

Mary Magdalene was shuddering so that the other Mary dared not speak to her, and her teeth were rattling in her head. But when they began to wrap him in the cloth, she crept closer, crouching down again like an animal and suddenly she leapt for the bier, and such a shout of agony burst from her throat that it seemed as if it must wake the two crucified thieves that had been left hanging. They had covered his face.

She did not touch him. She knelt there on the ground beside his shrouded body, with all the astonished men round her. And her hands hovered fearfully over the cloth that hid him and all her strong body was shaking silently now and they dared not touch her, because of the awful look on her face.

DESCENT FROM THE CROSS, Peter Paul Rubens (1577–1640), Musee des Beaux-Arts, © Erich Lessing/Art Resource, (ART86339).

LOVE STOOD AT A DISTANCE

Mary Borden

Who is this woman? Is she by chance of the family of the dead?"

"No, sir," the other Mary answered. "She is not of his kindred. She is only a follower. Jesus was her master. She came with us from Galilee in search of him."

"And you?"

"He was my husband's sister's child. I came with his mother to find him. But we were too late. We only saw him when he was crucified." . . .

It was growing dark. Mary Magdalene was still kneeling on the ground, her hands hovering over the shrouded figure and her body shaking. She didn't seem to be aware of anything round her. The men conferred together in low tones, then Joseph spoke again to the other Mary.

"You must take her away," he said. . . .

So Mary, the sister of Jesus' mother, went to Mary Magdalene and touched her on the shoulder and spoke to the shaking creature as if to a child and said:

"Come, they are going to bury him. Come, we will see where he is laid."

"But he is not dead. They must not bury him when he is not dead."

And now the men were exasperated. They said to themselves that they had to do with a mad woman, and the centurion was about to take her by the arm and drag her away, but Joseph of Arimathaea came forward and spoke kindly, saying:

"He was my friend, Mary of Magdala. I also loved him, and I am laying him to rest in a chamber of stone, hewn out of a rock in my garden that is close by. If you will follow us, you will see that he will be safe there and better than here in this gully. And he took her by the hands and lifted her to her feet, and she let him have his way."

So the soldiers carried him on the stretcher upon the bank and along the road, and a servant went before, carrying a lantern, and one walked to either side to give more light and the others followed with the two Marys behind the men.

> And all the people that came together to that sight, beholding the things which were done, smote their breasts, and returned. And all his acquaintance, and the women that followed him from Galilee, stood afar off, beholding these things. . . . There were also women looking on afar off: among whom was Mary Magdalene, and Mary the mother of James the less and of Joses, and Salome (LUKE 23:48–49; MARK 15:40).

CHRIST CARRIED TO THE TOMB, James J. Tissot (1839-1902). © SuperStock (999-324).

And they came to the new tomb that Joseph had had cut in the rock, and it was in a quiet garden and there was a sound of birds fluttering in the trees and the moon was rising behind the bushes as they put his body into the tomb and rolled a stone before the door of the tomb. And the two Marys stood in the shadow and saw where he was laid.

MARY OF MAGDALA

PAM KENNEDY

There were those, she supposed, who would call her possessed still. They would say she was captivated by her adoration of this strange Galilean just as she had been earlier in her life by seven evil spirits.

But Mary knew the difference. In those years before Jesus touched her, she had been driven past insanity—unloved and cast away from "good people." Then Jesus had passed through her town, little Magdala, on the western shores of Galilee. She didn't remember much of the encounter except that his cool, firm hand had touched her and the evil spirits had departed. She could think and speak and dream her own dreams again, and she wanted nothing more than to follow the one who had healed her. If that was possession, so be it.

Mary had joined two other women who traveled with Jesus, cooking meals and washing clothes. Others might have considered it menial; she considered it a privilege. By their acts of simple service they were able to hear his every word.

Mary assumed it would be her vocation for as long as she lived. It had not occurred to her that he would die first. But here she stood, surrounded by the crowd. On the crest of the hill, Jesus hung, bleeding and dying. And Mary could do nothing. She wanted to pray, but could not remember the words. She wanted to comfort his mother, but could not think how.

Through the day she remained, absorbing every sight and sound. She saw the darkness wrap itself around the city like a shroud. She felt the clammy heat of noon and the tremble of the earth. She heard the cry, "It is finished!" and watched as they took him off the cross.

The sky was beginning to dim as she hurried to the home of Salome, mother of James and John. Together they gathered precious oils and spices. They would observe the Sabbath, but the day after, at dawn, they would proceed to the tomb to render one last service to their Lord.

In the morning, as the sun lighted the east, Mary, Salome, and a few others stole through the quiet streets carrying their small pouch.

"Who will roll away the stone?" one whispered as they rounded the last corner. Mary looked up and gasped. The stone was moved!

Slowly they entered, fearful of what they might see. Before them was a young man in a white robe. The dazzling brightness of his garment filled the dark tomb with a diffused light.

The man told them not to fear. He said that Jesus was alive. With urgency, he ordered

THE REPENTANT MAGDALENE, James J. Tissot (1839–1902), © SuperStock (999–155).

them to go and tell the disciples. Then he vanished.

"Come!" Salome urged. They gathered their skirts and fled the tomb, eager to tell the men of their astounding encounter.

But when they reached the room where the disciples were hiding, the men laughed at them. "Women's hysterics," one observed. Peter, however, said nothing. He stood and motioned for John, and together they left the house in silence. Mary followed, remaining in the shadows.

John arrived at the tomb first, but he hesitated at the opening. Then Peter, panting from his run up the hill, rushed into the tomb. Mary waited, quietly watching from behind a gnarled olive tree. In a few moments, Peter and John emerged from the tomb, arguing over the meaning of what they had seen. Had someone stolen the body? Had Jesus risen from the dead?

They never saw Mary as they rushed back to tell the others what they had seen. Feeling abandoned, Mary wept. She stepped over to the tomb for one last look inside. Through her tears, she saw two young men. When one asked gently why she cried, she replied, "They have taken my Lord away and I do not know where they have put him." She looked at the men imploringly and saw their focus moved from her to something beyond.

Spinning around, fearful that the Roman soldiers had returned, Mary stood face to face with a man dressed in the simple clothes of a laborer. Supposing him to be the gardener, she hastily attempted to dry her eyes.

"Woman," said the stranger, "why are you crying? Who is it that you seek?"

"Oh please, sir, if you have carried away his body, please tell me where you have put him and I will get him."

The gardener's dark eyes softened, and a smile played at his lips. "Mary" was all that he said.

In that instant, she knew it was he! Joy pierced her heart. She fell at his feet, crying, "Teacher!"

Gently, he stroked her hair and then helped her to her feet. He explained to her how he must return to the Father, how she could not cling to him any longer. Seeing her despair, he assured her, however, that God would be forever with her as a father is with a beloved child. Then he told her to go and tell the disciples the good news.

Master and servant parted once more, but this time with joy, not sorrow. Mary's feet seemed to have wings as she ran to tell the disciples she had seen and talked to the Lord. Some listened to her tale and believed it; some still doubted. But this mattered little to Mary of Magdala. For she had seen and touched the living God, the resurrected Jesus. That was the reality. There was now hope after despair, laughter after tears, freedom after slavery. There was truly life after death.

MARY MAGDALENE

In the end of the sabbath, as it began to dawn toward the first day of the week, came Mary Magdalene and the other Mary to see the sepulchre. Now when Jesus was risen early the first day of the week, he appeared first to Mary Magdalene, out of whom he had cast seven devils (MATTHEW 28:1; MARK 16:9).

Mary Magdalene most likely came from Magdala, a city on the southwest coast of the Sea of Galilee. Scripture relates that Jesus cast out seven demons from her and she immediately became one of his followers.

Mary Magdalene has been associated with "a woman in the city, which was a sinner" who anoints Jesus' feet (Luke 7:37–38) and with the woman who was accused of adultery but was saved by Jesus from stoning. But Scripture does not support either. Because of these associations and because the Jewish Talmud ascribes a reputation for prostitution to the city of Magdala, Mary Magdalene is often thought to have been forgiven of these sins by Jesus. Whatever her shortcomings before she met the Master, her life after appears to have been one of unwavering faith.

Mary Magdalene was present at the trial of Jesus and she heard Pilate pronounce the sentence of death. She witnessed the humiliation and beatings of Jesus and was at the cross comforting both him and his mother. As the disciples were grieving, Mary Magdalene was on her way to the tomb to anoint the body and she was the one chosen by God to first receive the good news of Christ's resurrection. She was the first to arrive at the open tomb and the first to see the risen Christ.

Scripture does not mention Mary Magdalene after the resurrection, but she was probably among the women who gathered with the disciples in the Upper Room to await the anointing of the Holy Spirit. Mary Magdalene stands as an example of unwavering faith; after Jesus cast out the seven devils in her, she obviously never again doubted that he was who he said he was.

SPREADING THE GOOD NEWS

BY AN UNKNOWN DISCIPLE

As I stood grappling with my misery, I heard a gay voice singing and a woman in the blue clothing of a peasant turned the corner of the path and came towards me. It was Mary Magdalene. I looked at her in amazement. Were all women heartless as all men were cruel? Jesus was dead and the world was black to me, but the sunshine was still golden to her. And she had seemed to love him.

Mary came nearer and at the sight of my face her song stopped.

"How can you sing, Mary, when Jesus is dead?" I said, and turned to go, but she caught me by the sleeve.

"Jesus is not dead," she cried, and I stopped short, a wild, impossible hope springing upon me.

"What do you mean, Mary? I saw him die."

"And so did I. But I have seen him since," she said.

"Seen him? Are you mad?" I said.

She shook her head. "You have been ill. You have not heard. Sit down and I will tell you." So we sat down at the foot of the tree.

"You must see that something has happened," she said. "You cannot think that I could be so callous. I who loved him more

than any. Had I not more to love him for?"

Her eyes filled with tears, and she put her hand on my arm. . . .

"I was broken for days after his death. But look at me now. Am I the same woman who stood weeping beneath the cross, hopeless and in misery?"

"What has happened to you, Mary?" I asked. The dullness had settled on me again and I thought she raved.

"I have seen Jesus," she said. "At first I thought it was the gardener. But then I saw that it was Jesus."

"You were dreaming, Mary. You have deceived yourself," I said, but she shook her head and smiled.

"You think I cannot tell truth from dreams. And I tell you, no, I am not mad. Look at me and see if it is not true." I looked at her and indeed she seemed quite sane, but her talk was mad. "I saw Jesus alive still, and whereas I was in misery I am now full of joy."

"You have deceived yourself, Mary," I said again.

And she cried out vehemently, "Could I be happy if Jesus were really dead, if he were only a dreamer and his vision of the kingdom impossible? Others have seen him too. Men everywhere are asking what has happened to

NOLI ME TANGERE, Guiseppe B. Chairi (1654–1727) © Christie's Images/SuperStock (1100–869).

THE THREE MARYS AT THE TOMB, Jan van Eyck (c1390–1441), Museum Boymans van Beuningen, © Kavaler/Art Resource, (ART80974).

vent like a fire that burns. We cannot be unhappy." . . . And she went away and left me there under the tree of God.

It was in Galilee, on the mountain where I had first heard Jesus teach, that hope came back to me. After a hard day's work I had wandered away from the village and climbed the mountain and sat looking down on the great plain with its vineyards and olive gardens and the thin gray smoke that rose in the air as the women made ready the evening meal. The voices of the children driving the cattle home came from the plain, and far in the distance a cow lowed to her calf and the sheep baaed to their lambs. Darkness was falling, but I could not go. The light faded and blackness covered the land. I bowed my head on my arms and sat, too tired for sleep, too hopeless for pain, too sad for tears. The wild beasts cried aloud in the night, but I did not move. All night I sat there, and in the morning came the dawn.

us. When you see Peter and John again you can judge for yourself. . . . Our minds are fer-

First there came the stillness. No bird cheeped, no wild beast cried aloud. A faint glimmer of light showed the dark masses of the forests on the hills and the dim silver line of the sea. The golden light spread and touched the land, and color awoke again in earth and sky. The sun came up behind the mountains and the shadows lay from east to west along the plain. It was then that the vision came to me. I saw nothing. I heard nothing, but as the dawn spread slowly over the land, waking the earth to beauty, something awoke in my heart. I do not know what it was. I have no words to tell of it. The earth lay before me bathed in a light that men seldom see, a clear radiance that transormed each familiar place and gave the world the beauty of a dream. And yet it was still the earth. The forests and moors, the mountains and valleys, were the same, but another light lay upon them. So it was with my soul. An intense, still joy awoke in my heart, a joy in which there was no shadow of restlessness or disturbance, and the old gay sense of something added to life came back to me. It seemed as though Jesus had watched by me all night and I had not known it. The place was full of his presence.

The glory of the vision blinded me, and I hid my eyes. There was no death. Each night the beauty of the earth died into darkness, each dawn in wonder the light rose again on it. It was so with the spirit of man. In tribulation and in agony happiness died, but in beauty and glory, joy lived again. I rolled over on my face on the coarse mountain grass and lay there thinking. The greatest miracle in the world had happened to me. A remembrance of beauty and love and immortal passion, the romance of the earth and of life had taken hold of me. The smallest, meanest things had gained a power of signifying the greatest, noblest things. The world was full of wonders. Nothing was impossible for love.

The children had begun to drive the cattle out. Their shrill cries rose in the air before I stirred. When I sat up and looked at the earth again it was broad, garish day. The beauty of the world no longer took my breath away. In the bustle of life my vision must fade, but I did not mind. I had seen the eternal beauty that lies hidden in the commonplace. There was a work to do, and like Peter and the disciples I must do it, no matter the cost. I rose to my feet to go back to my village and take up my job again.

JOANNA AND SALOME
THE EMPTY TOMB

TOYOHIKO KAGAWA

As they climbed the slope to the sepulcher, the four women went, in unspoken accord, more slowly. The journey through Jerusalem's narrow and deserted streets had been black and desolate beyond the telling. They had reached the outskirts of the city when a sharp earthquake occurred and the sky overhead took on a strange, unfamiliar color. They had huddled together for long frightened moments, rolling eyes upward at the great heaped clouds and feeling the road tremble as if with palsy. Salome had suggested turning back, but Mary Magdalene would have none of it. With resolution now she led the way up the twisting path to the garden of Joseph of Arimathea, a dark silent figure in the gloom. Salome and Mary, the mother of James, wept and moaned a little as they mounted the incline, their grief steady and resigned. All rebellion had gone out of them when they had watched with Jesus' mother at the foot of the cross. Only the sorrow, deep and beyond human stemming, remained.

Joanna, like Mary Magdalene, could not weep. A great heaviness was upon her, the weight of spirit and of body and of the night. Her thoughts were slow as words thickly spoken in alien tongue. Her feet dragged as if shackled. The jars of spices which she bore were an almost intolerable burden. She could go no farther. She could not. Yet she must. She, with those faithful others, must minister to the broken body of the Master.

"But who will roll us away the stone from before the sepulcher?" wailed Salome in sudden anxiety.

"Perhaps the guards will help us when they see we mean no trouble," said Mary, the mother of James.

Joanna thought of the size of the boulder. "It will take at least three score."

Only Mary Magdalene said nothing. Rounding a group of thick-leaved trees, they stopped. There were lights in the garden ahead, and much confusion. Nay, there was one light, a strange radiance from the sepulcher. Soldiers were running toward them, away from the tomb. Others stood huddled together in groups. Some knelt with faces covered, sobbing like children.

Joanna was stricken with consternation. The stone was rolled away from the cave's mouth! Father in heaven, what had happened? She started forward with her companions. No voice challenged them. None of the guards

MARY MAGDALENE IN THE TOMB, James J. Tissot (1836-1902). © SuperStock (999-430).

made any attempt to halt them.

Mary Magdalene was first at the sepulcher. Joanna followed her, stooping down to look into the cavern. She heard Mary Magdalene's quick intake of breath, and then she herself felt the quickening of her startled heart. The body of Jesus was not there!

The jar of sweet ointment fell from Joanna's nerveless hands with a crash. She looked down blindly at the shattered pieces on the cave's floor, and fragrance drifted up to her slowly. Her throat was painfully tight. Her two fists ached. Was it not enough that they had crucified him? Could they not let the dead rest in peace?

Beside her, she heard Salome breathe: "Behold!"

She lifted her head and through eyes blurred with moisture saw, in the dimness of the tomb, two white figures, one at the head and one at the foot, where the body of Jesus had lain.

For the shaking of her lips, Joanna could utter no sound. Nor could she look longer upon the figures, for the strange glistening of their raiment.

There came a voice from the sepulcher, and it was like no voice which Joanna had ever heard.

"Fear not: for I know

There were also women looking on afar off: among whom was Mary Magdalene, and Mary the mother of James the less and of Joses, and Salome; (Who also, when he was in Galilee, followed him, and ministered unto him;) and many other women which came up with him unto Jerusalem (MARK 15:40–41).

you seek Jesus which was crucified. He is not here, for he is risen, as he said. Go quickly and tell his disciples that he goes before you into Galilee. There shall you see him. Lo, I have told you."

When Joanna came to herself, she was with Salome and Mary the mother of James hastening along the road back to Jerusalem. How or when she had left the sepulcher, she knew not. Only one thing she knew. They must find Peter and John and the others. They must tell them of the astounding events.

Salome said suddenly: "But—but where is Mary Magdalene?"

"Is she not with us?" asked Joanna. She turned her head, half expecting to see a figure hurrying to overtake them. But there was naught upon that road but the pale dawn.

Mary Magdalene could not leave. She stood outside of the sepulcher and the tears she could not shed before fell now. She was frightened, bewildered, and, above everything, desolate. In her agony, she knew not what to think. Were those gleaming figures in the sepulcher part of a dream or vision, or were they representatives of evil men who had robbed the tomb of the body of her beloved master? She walked blindly

CHRIST'S TOMB, Jerusalem, Israel © R.Opfer/H. Armstrong Roberts (KR-64547).

in the garden, not able to see her way because of tears. She stumbled into bushes. Branches caught at her garments, and she bruised her sandaled feet on sharp, upthrusting stones. Dimly, she was aware of a man approaching and turned a little away from him, bowing her face in her hands.

"Woman," said the stranger, "why do you weep?"

She did not answer. Why did she weep? There was reason in plenty. None, she moaned inwardly, had ever known such cause for grief. She had been thrust from a height into a pit where no light came and out of which she could never climb.

"Whom do you seek?"

The man's voice seemed to her far away, and she wished that he would go away and leave her with her sorrow.

Yet, he might know something of what had occurred here. Perhaps he was the gardener.

"Sir," she said pleadingly, "if you have borne him hence, tell me where you have laid him, and I will take him away."

"Mary!"

That voice! That voice of infinite compassion. That tone of tender rebuke. Father in heaven, who was it spoke thus to her—who? She turned, shaking from bead to foot, and blinked the tears from her eyes.

"Rabboni!"

It was he! It was the Master! It was Jesus of Nazareth. Joy crowded into her heart. There was room for naught else. She flung herself forward to touch him, to hold him. . . .

Jesus said to her: "Touch me not, for I am not yet ascended to my Father; but go to my brethren, and say to them that I ascend to my Father and your Father; and to my God, and your God."

Mary Magdalene sank to her knees in the dew-wet grass, and her prayer had no words, for it needed none. . . . When she lifted her head, Jesus had disappeared. Nevertheless, she doubted not that she had indeed seen him, and returned to Jerusalem with rejoicing to seek out the disciples.

JOANNA AND SALOME

John Evangelist Walsh

It was the morning after the council meeting, just about sunrise. I was in bed upstairs. There came a loud, rapid knocking at the main door, then there was a subdued mutter of women's voices, several of them and all talking at once, but in lowered tones. No doubt Sarah, thinking I was asleep, had uttered a caution. I was not asleep. I had hardly slept all night except for a wink here and there. Seconds later Sarah was at my door, knocking softly and peeking in. I said yes, I was awake, what was it?

"Joanna is here and she's very upset. She came only for a moment. She says they were at the tomb this morning." Seeing me throw back the covers she paused, then added, "She'll tell you herself." I took my robe and we went down. . . .

Joanna stood up and looked straight at me as I entered the lamplit sitting room, her eyes wide, nervous anxiety playing over her features. She always did have an expressive face. "Oh, sir!" she burst out, coming toward me with her hand reaching. "The body is gone! It's not there! What has happened, what shall we do?"

"Gone? Who?"

"We saw the place in the tomb. The body's not there!"

"Joanna, please sit down. There, now be calm. Tell me slowly." I poured her some water but she ignored it.

"We went to the tomb this morning, you know, as we were supposed to. Early, just before sunup. It was open so we went right in, all the way. And there was nothing there. No body at all. just empty! Who could have taken him? Why should anyone do such an awful thing?"

Her agitation, growing as she talked, was having its effect on my wife and daughters, for they stood staring at her, wide-eyed, the two girls with hands to their mouths. I was less affected by her excitement, but only because the truth dawned on me right in the middle of her breathless tale.

"Joanna, was Magdalene with you?"

"Yes. I mean no. We all started together from the house, but some of us waited to buy spices and we told Mary we'd catch up. She didn't want to stop, so she went ahead."

"By herself?"

"I think so. Yes, she did. She's like that."

"And the rest of you came along a few minutes later?"

"Not long. Ten minutes."

"And did you find her there at the tomb?"

Plainly, this was the first time the thought

THE THREE MARYS AT THE TOMB, Annibale Carracci (1560–1609) Hermitage,
St. Petersburg, Russia, © Scala/Art Resource (ART20253).

There were also women looking on afar off: among whom was
Mary Magdalene, and Mary the mother of James the less and of
Joses, and Salome; (Who also, when he was in Galilee, followed
him, and ministered unto him;) and many other women which came
up with him unto Jerusalem. It was Mary Magdalene, and Joanna,
and Mary the mother of James, and other women that were with
them, which told these things unto the apostles. And their words
seemed to them as idle tales, and they believed them not (MARK
15:40–41; LUKE 24:10–11).

THE THREE MARYS AT THE TOMB, Romolo Liverani (c.1809–1872), San Marco, Florence, Italy. © Nicolo Orsi Battaglini/Art Resource, (ART84872).

had occurred to the girl. She looked at me quizzically a few seconds before answering. "No, we didn't, but . . ."

"Joanna, my dear girl," I said, trying not to smile too broadly, "don't you see what happened? You and your friends went to the wrong tomb!"

That suggestion stopped her for a moment; her lips parted as she was about to speak. Then she went on, spreading her hands in a gesture of insistence. "No, no, how could that be? We were all at Golgotha, watching. We saw the place where you and Joseph put him, we all knew."

She glanced round uncertainly at Sarah and the girls, her smooth brow wrinkling and a shade of doubt in her eyes. Yet I could see that she wasn't convinced. "Oh, there was someone there," she said, turning back to

"He was a stranger. Salome asked while we were running off, and everyone said he was a stranger. I didn't see him too well except for the white clothes. But I could tell he had no beard. All of our men have beards."

"You're sure there was no one else?"

"Yes, sir, no one. . . ."

I turned to Sarah and said we'd go to the tomb and finish the task ourselves, all of us, including the girls.

"Please, Sarah, after yesterday you needn't worry about me being mixed up in it. Who doesn't know by now that I helped to bury him? Please?"

Her mouth softened and her eyelids slowly descended as she let out a small sigh. Then in a resigned tone she answered, "All right, Nico," and she turned to face Naomi and Rebecca. Quietly she fired off instructions that sent each running from the room in a different direction. Then she called Joanna over and gave more orders. "We'll be ready in half an hour," she said over her shoulder as she urged Joanna ahead of her out the door.

me. I forgot. A young man. He spoke, but Salome and I were behind the other women a little, so we couldn't hear. Anyway, we didn't know him."

"Where did you see this man?"

"Right at the tomb. When Salome and I got there, the others were all rushing out, and I saw him inside. Not all the way in. He was standing in the door of the vestibule. I could see his white clothes in the shadows."

"You're sure nobody recognized him?"

THE WOMEN AT THE TOMB

JOHN EVANGELIST WALSH

When I saw that the closure stone appeared to be standing well off-center, my reaction was prompted more by logic than anything else. Halting abruptly in my tracks, I looked around. "That can't be the one," I said. "We took a wrong turn from the path. The tomb is further."

Sarah, shading her eyes from the sun and staring hard, disagreed. "No, Nico, this is Joseph's tomb. But look, it's open."

The five of us hurried forward. Pausing outside the vestibule, we all stared. The large stone had indeed been rolled entirely to one side, to the left. The low entrance into the burial chamber was uncovered, completely open, with the bright sunlight creeping into the chamber along the earthen floor.

Four quick steps carried me across the vestibule. As I bent over, reaching hastily for the sides of the low entrance, my sandal caught on the hem of my robe, and my momentum brought me stumbling to the ground. Dropping my hands before me, I crawled on through, painfully aware of the pebbly dirt grinding into the flesh of my knees.

Inside I quickly raised up, still kneeling, and turned my head to look at the niche on the right, where we had placed the shrouded body. It was empty. I could see nothing at all on the stone bench. "Nico?" Sarah called anxiously from outside. "What is it? What do you see?"

I turned and looked at the niche in the rear wall. It was empty. I swung to the left. That niche was empty, too. I got to my feet. Stooping over the slab in the right-hand niche where we had placed the body, I ran my hand up and down the surface of the stone bench. Nothing, except for the sticky remains of the spices. . . .

"Nico?"

Groping backward across the chamber, I sat down on the stone slab of a niche. Numbly I stared at the dirt floor. I was dumbfounded to think that, against all common sense, Caiaphas had been right. His Galilean followers, of course. Who else would have an interest in the body of this man urgent enough to risk violating a tomb? But how in the name of heaven had they managed it? Only then did I remember the Roman guards.

"Nico, it's gone!" Sarah was crouching in the doorway.

"Yes, yes, it's gone. Did you see any of the guards out there? Where are the guards? Let me pass."

Outside, I stood at the vestibule door and swept my eyes carefully around the whole area. There was no one in sight, no sound. The centurion's tent, too, was missing from under the trees. I stepped out and hurried round to the north side of the high, spreading hill. Climbing a little way up the lower slope, I stopped and looked. Not another soul in the vicinity. I cast my eyes higher. Above me at the wide summit I saw the three empty crosses still looming, lifted up stark and black against the pale blue of the sky. Hateful instruments, I thought, lifted up like that. They should already have been removed and broken up, but a professional soldier will never do that kind of job unless he's given a direct order.

Lifted up—the phrase stirred in my memory—lifted up. Where had I heard those words before? Yes, he used them the night of my visit last year—but how? Try as I might to recall it, the memory stayed tantalizingly just out of reach as I turned and walked back down the rocky slope. . . .

"Tell me, Joanna, I've been wondering. How did you women expect to get into the tomb? There were no men with you to move the stone. At least you mentioned none."

"Oh, that was all mixed up. We'd forgotten about it, except for Salome. We were almost here when someone remembered and said we wouldn't be able to get in. But you know there are men, the gardener and his helpers, who take care of this whole place, the tombs and the plants and trees. Salome told us she'd already sent them a message, and we'd wait till they came."

"How many women were with you?"

"There were five. Six if you count Magdalene."

"And what brought you so quickly to my house? You must have come almost straight from here."

"The others said I should."

"Where were the women going when you left them?"

"They went to tell Peter."

"What about Magdalene? You and the others didn't see her. Where do you think she went?"

"I wonder about that. Maybe she saw the empty tomb and then went back another way. She's very brave, but I'm sure she would have been as frightened as we were. And she was alone."

"The young man you saw, the stranger. Dressed in white, you say. Is that so very unusual?"

"Not just white. You know the way the moon sometimes has a glow around it? Like that. But now I'm not so sure, I mean with the darkness and the shadows and the bright torch and everything, and all of us running away so scared."

The troubled look that had gradually come over her face seemed to say that there would be little value in further questioning. In any case, there were several things I wanted to accomplish, and without more loss of time.

"Joanna, you must do me a favor, if you

THE THREE MARYS AT THE TOMB, Bartolomeo Schedoni (c.1570–1615), Galleria Nazionale, Parma, Italy. © Scala/Art Resource (ART80465).

will. Do you know where Magdalene lives?"

"Yes."

"Run and find her. Have her come to my house. Say I want to ask her about this morning. I think she'll come, but if she refuses, then tell her—in a nice way, mind you—that as an officer of the council I require her attendance." She pulled her veil tight under her chin with one hand, gathered her skirts with the other, and ran off.

To Sarah and the girls I said we would shortly be returning to the city. Meanwhile I wanted to have another look around inside the tomb. They waited in the vestibule to escape the sun, still talking.

Inside I sat down on the left-hand stone bench, opposite where the body had lain. Dumbly I looked at the earthen floor, shaking my head. . . . I had been gazing down in an abstracted way at the chamber floor. Now I became aware that the light, dry soil was considerably scuffed about. . . . I did recognize several thick, square-toed impressions as typically those of a Roman officer. This would have been Centurion Vinucius, when he came in to check on the body that first day. The only mark of real interest that I could find showed about half of a right sandal, a bit larger than ordinary, larger than mine. . . . A vague X-shaped mark could be seen near the toe, probably a repair, and a thin, shallow crack split the sole near its center. . . .

I stood up when Sarah spoke from the entrance, her voice urgent. "Nico! Nico! Magdalene is here."

Ducking through the doorway, I saw her from the vestibule. She was approaching from the left, still forty or fifty feet away, walking quite slowly. Her usually upright carriage was sadly slumped, and long wisps of her abundant black hair straggled before her face. Her eyes fixed on the ground, she didn't look up until she came near. Then as she turned into the vestibule, she gave a start at finding us standing there, and her head lifted abruptly. Red eyes and glistening cheeks made it plain she'd been crying. . . .

"Mary, thank you for coming. But I told Joanna to have you go to my house. I didn't mean to bring you out here."

"Joanna?"

"Didn't Joanna tell you I was looking for you?"

"No." Her voice sounded flat and contained a note of dejection. I was sorry to see her face so drawn.

"Tell me, Mary, why have you come back? Weren't you here this morning early?" Her reply scarcely answered my question. She seemed almost to be talking to herself.

"They wouldn't believe me when I told them the body was missing. They said I must have been at the wrong tomb. I knew I was at the right tomb. But they said I couldn't have been." Suddenly she looked straight at me. "You know his body is gone; you were inside. Who has taken it?" Nervously she lifted both hands to her face, wiping at her cheeks.

"Mary, exactly what happened out here this morning?"

"I came ahead of the others. The tomb was open and I saw the body was gone, so I ran back and told Peter and John. They just said I should sit down and rest. Then I went and told the others and none of them would listen either." . . . But you see I was right, this time I was right. He's not in there, is he? Please go and tell them. They'll believe you."

"You saw nothing else this morning; no guards?"

"Guards? Why should there be guards? No, there was nothing else, no one."

It was obvious that she was too upset to be questioned further, nor was it likely that she had much more to tell. Suggesting that, in her state she shouldn't be out here alone, I invited her to return to the city with us. Shaking her head she turned away. She'd stay at the tomb a little while, she murmured, then go home and see if they'd believe her this time.

> Then came to him the mother of Zebedee's children with her sons, worshipping him, and desiring a certain thing of him. And he said unto her, What wilt thou? She saith unto him, Grant that these my two sons may sit, the one on thy right hand, and the other on the left, in thy kingdom. But Jesus answered and said, Ye know not what ye ask. Are ye able to drink of the cup that I shall drink of, and to be baptized with the baptism that I am baptized with? They say unto him, We are able. . . . And when the sabbath was past, Mary Magdalene, and Mary the mother of James, and Salome, had bought sweet spices, that they might come and anoint him (MATTHEW 20:20–22; MARK 16:1).

JOANNA

Joanna was the wife of Chuza who was the steward of Herod Antipas. Luke tells us that she and Susanna gave their own money for the earthly needs of Jesus and his disciples. Joanna accompanied Mary Magdalene to the tomb and then to tell the disciples of the resurrection of Jesus. Joanna is only mentioned by Luke, and some scholars believe that she may have been one of the physician's sources for the Gospel of Luke.

SALOME

Salome was the wife of Zebedee and the mother of James and John, the "sons of Thunder." When she asked Jesus to grant her sons special favors, he explained to her that she didn't understand the sacrifices that would be required. But Salome proved faithful to the Master. She was at the crucifixion even though at least one of her sons, James, seemed not to be present. She came to the tomb to anoint the body and was one of the first to see that the stone had been rolled away. Scripture doesn't tell us more about Salome, but one can only imagine her excitement as she ran to tell her sons that Jesus had risen from the dead.

APPARITION OF CHRIST TO THE THREE MARYS, Laurent de La Hyre (1606–1656),
Louvre, Paris, France. © Erich Lessing/Art Resource.(ART6324).

SUSANNA

THE OTHER WOMAN AT THE TOMB

PAM KENNEDY

The morning was dark and damp as the women scurried along silently through the sleeping streets. Susanna clutched the bundle of aromatic spices tightly, the scent of myrrh winding about her like a funeral shroud. She shuddered. She didn't want to be here, not like this. As the pale fingers of the dawn crept along the distant hill, the birds began to call to each other. To Susanna they sounded like cries of warning. Her heart pounded. Her lungs ached. Her head throbbed.

"Hurry," Mary of Magdala called over her shoulder.

"But what if there are soldiers?" the other Mary cried in a gasping whisper. "And what about the stone?"

Susanna's mind raced backwards even as her feet swept across the dewy weeds. How could it have come to this? Only weeks ago she had followed the Master, drinking in his words like a parched desert drinks in water. Ever since his touch had healed her, she had trailed after him, hauling cool water, bringing bread and barley cakes, running errands for the disciples. Once destitute and empty, her life finally had meaning and purpose. Only seven days ago, in the streets of Jerusalem, she had seen her master hailed as king. Even now, the memory brought a thrill of joy. But as suddenly as thunderclouds on a summer day, events had tumbled and crashed about her. The Master was arrested, tried, mocked, crucified, buried, and it was all over. Ended. Hope was as dead as the body they had carried from the cross.

Tears traced their familiar paths down Susanna's cheeks. How could Mary do it? What kept her determined? This was foolish. They could all be killed. Suddenly, Mary stopped and Susanna nearly fell against her. The small group of women stood panting in the velvety shadows of a huge acacia.

"Look!" Susanna's whisper rang with awe.

The women stared. Ahead of them, like a gaping black wound, stood the open tomb.

The heavy stone, intended to seal the crypt, was pushed aside. There were no guards, no soldiers, no sounds but the sighing breezes and the crying birds.

Mary Magdalene walked

And Joanna the wife of Chuza Herod's steward, and Susanna, and many others, which ministered unto him of their substance (LUKE 8:3).

slowly forward toward the opening, never taking her eyes from the blackness within. Susanna felt drawn, almost against her will, to follow. She reached to grasp the other Mary's hand—as cold and clammy as her own—and together they edged toward the tomb.

Susanna wanted to run away; away from the dark, cold, death-drenched place, back to the city where life throbbed with color and sound. But she stayed, compelled by something stronger than herself.

Slowly, the women entered the cool dimness of the tomb. Once inside they stood paralyzed with wonder, filled with fear.

"Don't be frightened." The voice was deep and resonant, full of strength, yet tempered with kindness. Light radiated from the speaker, a young man robed in dazzling white.

Susanna stared at the earthen floor of the tomb, fearful of meeting the piercing gaze of the speaker.

"Why do you seek the living among the dead?" he asked. "Don't you recall Jesus said he would rise again from the dead?"

The two questions rang in Susanna's ears and echoed in her heart. She dared a glance at the unearthly stranger and his eyes caught hers and held them.

SLEEPING GUARDS, RESURRECTION (detail), Piero della Francesca (c.1420–1492), Pinacoteca Comunale. © Erich Lessing/Art Resource (ART 92205).

"Go now and tell the others. He is risen. You shall see him again."

Susanna's heart pounded. Alive? The Master was alive!

Mary Magdalene's urgency cut through Susanna's awe. "Come! Come quickly!"

The others were already outside, dashing like children down the dawn-pink road. Susanna turned once more to the tomb. The stranger was gone. The light had faded. The tomb was dark.

But in her heart, she had captured the brilliance of the words "He is risen." The death knell was silenced, the night of grief was past, and in the freshness of the shining dawn, Susanna discovered the truth at last. The tomb was not the end of it all. It was only the beginning.

SUSANNA

And . . . Susanna, and many others, which ministered unto him of their substance (LUKE 8:3).

There is only one mention of Susanna in the Bible. This passage tells us a lot about her and the other women, but it also tantalizes us with what it does not say. Susanna is one of the women who followed Jesus. Susanna, like Joanna, gave of her own money to provide for the earthly needs of Jesus and his disciples. That leaves us with questions as to where Susanna might have gotten the money. Did she have a wealthy husband? Was he also a follower of Jesus? We can speculate that the women cooked the food and cleaned the clothes of the Master as well as providing financial assistance.

RUINS OF A SYNAGOGUE IN CAPERNAUM, ON THE SEA OF GALILEE. © H. Armstrong Roberts (KR 111926).

BENEATH THE CROSS

FATEFUL MEETINGS

And Pilate answered and said again unto them, What will ye then that I shall do unto him whom ye call the King of the Jews? And they cried out again, Crucify him. Then Pilate said unto them, Why, what evil hath he done? And they cried out the more exceedingly, Crucify him. And so Pilate, willing to content the people, released Barabbas unto them, and delivered Jesus, when he had scourged him, to be crucified (MARK 15:12–15).

A WOMAN WIPES THE FACE OF JESUS, James J. Tissot (1836–1902). ©SuperStock (999-395).

MALCHUS

MALCHUS, THE WOUNDED ENEMY

Walter Kortrey

As the years went by, Malchus must have recalled that night in the garden. Whenever in rain or cold, he felt the faint throbbing in that scar on his ear, the whole scene must have flashed again upon the wide screen of his memory. Then he would think, with a wry smile, of Simon Peter's clumsy swordsmanship and, in greater depth, of the living word of love with which Jesus had touched him.

Malchus remembered how, when they came to Gethsemane, he had worked his way to the front of the temple contingent, watching for Iscariot and his kiss signal. Then just when he had expected a chase through the garden, the Nazarene, in complete command of himself and of the situation, had come forward, saying, "Who is it you are looking for? Here I am!"

After that it was all confusion. Malchus remembered watching Simon struggling to get his borrowed sword out of its sheath. The hilt caught in his waistband, and it was plain to see that he was new at the game. At any rate, he didn't scare anybody. There was a lot of noise and distraction, scuffling and shouting among the Nazarene's men, and then suddenly, out of the torchlight smoke, Simon came like a charging bull lunging toward them.

They all scattered, laughing and catcalling as they ducked and hit the ground. But Simon's temper was up and his sword lashed out, thrusting and thrashing in a crazy, haphazard way. Malchus remembered trying to get out of range and the quick sharp pain and wet warmth of his own blood on his neck.

Malchus remembered how Jesus had come to him then, with comfort and healing in his hands. The blood stopped flowing, the pain over his whole right side began to subside, and Malchus knew that his life would never be the same again.

In later years, running his finger over the old scar, Malchus remembered how Jesus had given meaning and truth to his own incredible commandment, "Love your enemy. Do good to those who hate you. Bless those who curse you. Pray for those who mistreat you; love your enemies and do good to them."

Malchus had felt in his own body the possibility of Jesus' impossible idea. The very words, "love your enemy," had come alive for him in the healing of his own wounds. There in the garden on the Mount of Olives, the high priest's servant caught a glimpse of love through the eyes of God. "Greater love has no man than this, that he give up his life for his friend."

MALCHUS

Then Simon Peter having a sword drew it, and smote the high priest's servant, and cut off his right ear. The servant's name was Malchus. And Jesus answered and said, Suffer ye thus far. And he touched his ear, and healed him (JOHN 18:10; LUKE 22:51).

In the Garden of Gethsemane, at the arrest of Jesus, the high priest Caiaphas was represented by his slave Malchus. The first-century a.d. historian Josephus writes that servants of the high priest were known to represent their master in particularly unpleasant situations. Some scholars suggest that Malchus may have been a Nabataean Arab from the deserts east and south of Judea, since Malchus was a common Nabataean name. Malchus is never again mentioned in Scripture, but the healing of his ear stands in Biblical history as the supreme example of "love your enemies."

CHRIST HEALING THE EAR OF MALCHUS, James J. Tissot (1836–1902). © SuperStock (999-239).

BARABBAS
BARABBAS PONDERS

Pär Lagerkvist

There wasn't anyone who rose from the dead, neither their adored "Master" nor anyone else! And besides, he, Barabbas, could hardly be blamed for their choice. That was their business. They could have chosen anyone at all, but it just turned out that way. The Son of God! As if he could be the Son of God! But supposing he were, there was surely no need for him to have been crucified if he had not wanted to be. He must have wanted it himself. There was something weird and horrid about it—he must have wanted to suffer. For if he really was the Son of God, it would have been the easiest thing in the world to get out of it. But he didn't want to get out of it. He wanted to suffer and die in that dreadful way and not be spared; and so it had been; he had gotten his own way about not being let off. He had let him, Barabbas, go free instead. He had commanded: "Release Barabbas and crucify me."

Though of course he was not the Son of God, that was obvious. . . . He had used his power in the most extraordinary way. Used it by not using it, as it were; allowed others to decide exactly as they liked; refrained from interfering and yet had gotten his own way all the same: to be crucified instead of Barabbas.

They spoke of his having died for them. That might be. But he really had died for Barabbas, no one could deny it! In actual fact, he was closer to him than they were, closer than anyone else, was bound up with him in quite another way. Although they didn't want to have anything to do with him. He was chosen, one might say, chosen to escape suffering, to be let off. He was the real chosen one, acquitted instead of the Son of God himself—at his command, because he wished it. Though they suspected nothing!

And they had then a notable prisoner, called Barabbas. Therefore when they were gathered together, Pilate said unto them, Whom will ye that I release unto you? Barabbas, or Jesus which is called Christ? For he knew that for envy they had delivered him (Matthew 27:16–18).

BARABBAS

And they cried out all at once, saying, Away with this man, and release unto us Barabbas: (Who for a certain sedition made in the city, and for murder, was cast into prison.) . . . And he released unto them him that for sedition and murder was cast into prison, whom they had desired; but he delivered Jesus to their will (LUKE 23:18–19, 25).

Arrested for the crimes of insurrection and murder, Barabbas was released when the crowd chose him to be released and Jesus, the Christ, to be crucified. There is no further mention in Scripture of Barabbas after his release.

BARABBAS, James J. Tissot (1836-1902), © SuperStock (999-9269).

Caiaphas and Annas
The Voice of Caiaphas

Robert Hoyer

It was really too bad we had to hold a trial at all, but these laws we have made it impossible for sensible people simply to kill off a dangerous radical like Jesus. The trial was a mockery. It was purely political, and we had to make it appear holy. I suppose it was technically illegal, but its result was good. A man must often act out a sham to make the people follow for their own good. Believe me, I know; that's what made that year's job tough. I had to act as the high priest of a God I neither know nor want. I stood in the temple daily, acting. . . . Now don't hold up your hands in horror—why should I be ashamed of it? Someone had to lead the blind, the uneducated. I think I put on a pretty good act. I had Jesus condemned as a blasphemer. . . . I was the only one who went through with it just because I knew Jesus had to be killed, and I had to act as though I were doing it as a servant of God. If I weren't able to laugh at it all, it would have been even harder. Even Judas provided

some comedy. He came and asked for forgiveness. Ha! I told him: "What is it to us, if you want forgiveness—that's your concern, not ours!"

What I did was right, that's clear; in spite of your resurrection fables. Why, think what would have happened if I had changed my mind and become a follower of your amateur preacher at the last moment. I could have declared Jesus innocent, and disbanded the council. That's a laugh, too. My father-in-law, Annas, and the council would have overruled me and killed Jesus without me. I think they would have botched that business with Pilate, and brought reprisals from Rome. And I would have been disgraced, deposed, stripped of my wealth, banished from Jerusalem, possibly stoned and killed. That's good? Then all I'd have today would be Jesus' forgiveness—nothing but your "inner peace and happiness and glory and strength." No, thanks. I'd have to hope for heaven, if I'd been gentle with your leader.

> Then assembled together the chief priests, and the scribes, and the elders of the people, unto the palace of the high priest, who was called Caiaphas, And consulted that they might take Jesus by subtlety, and kill him. . . . And they that had laid hold on Jesus led him away to Caiaphas the high priest, where the scribes and the elders were assembled. (Matthew 26:3–4, 57).

CAIAPHAS AND ANNAS

And Annas the high priest, and Caiaphas, and John, and Alexander, and as many as were of the kindred of the high priest, were gathered together at Jerusale (ACTS 4:6).

Annas was born into a wealthy and influential family and as the head of the most prominent high priestly family, Annas was at the very pinnacle of Jewish aristocracy. He was a man of wealth and education and was a leader of the Sanhedrin. He and his family had collaborated with Roman rule and were leading Sadducees.

About A.D. 6 or 7, Quirinius, governor of Syria, appointed Annas as high priest. About eight years later, he was deposed by Valerius Gratus, the procurator of Judea, but Annas continued to be the most influential of the priests and continued to be known as the high priest.

After his removal, Annas was succeeded by each of his five sons, one grandson, and his son-in-law Caiaphas, who presided at Jesus' trial. Jesus was taken first to Annas who then sent him to Caiaphas. Annas and Caiaphas were still around during the Acts of the Apostles and they were the principal interrogators of Peter and John when they were arrested.

CHRIST BEFORE THE HIGH PRIEST, Gerrit van Honthorst (1590-1656), National Gallery, London, England. © National Gallery, London/SuperStock (900-100325).

PONTIUS PILATE
PILATE'S WIFE

FRANK SLAUGHTER

Dawn had broken long before Joseph's swift camel entered the courtyard of Herod's palace in Jericho where Claudia Procula was staying. But the guard was a member of Pilate's household troops and knew him, so he was admitted immediately. The nomenclator informed him that the procurator's lady was still asleep, but at Joseph's insistence she was awakened. A few minutes later Claudia Procula came into the room, wrapped in a rich dressing robe, her face still flushed from sleep. When she saw who her visitor was, her eyes widened and her hand went to her breast. "Why are you here, Joseph!" she cried. "Is Pontius . . ."

"The procurator is in good health, I am told." He knelt before her. "I come to beg that you save Jesus of Nazareth."

"To save Jesus? What has happened?"

"Caiaphas arrested him for blasphemy and they have condemned him to death. The procurator will pass sentence on him today."

"Crucifixion!" she gasped.

"It is the Roman method of execution."

"But why? I thought they had decided he was harmless."

"Caiaphas fears Jesus," Joseph explained, "lest his teachings break the hold the high priest has on the people. He must have convinced the procurator that Jesus' death is best for the state."

Claudia Procula's eyes fell. "He required little convincing, Joseph. Pontius ordered me not to listen to Jesus and I refused. That is why I did not come to Jerusalem."

"You must come now," he urged, "or your husband will crucify the Son of God."

She looked at him closely and saw that he was confident of the truth in what he said. "I know Mary has believed he is the Messiah for a long time," she said. "But I did not think you believed it. What made you change your mind, Joseph?"

"This morning it was revealed to me," he told her simply. "I no longer doubt."

Her face grew pale. "Pontius must not do this thing, Joseph!" she cried. "Go order a chariot made ready. We will drive at once to Jerusalem."

They went directly to

When he was set down on the judgment seat, his wife sent unto him, saying, Have thou nothing to do with that just man: for I have suffered many things this day in a dream because of him (MATTHEW 27:19).

MESSAGE FROM PILATE'S WIFE, James J. Tissot (1836-1902), © SuperStock (999-9260).

Procula's apartment and found Mary waiting there. As the two women embraced, Claudia asked, "What must I do to stop this terrible thing, Mary?"

"Jesus is before the procurator now in the praetorium," Mary told her. "If you go to him be might still order a lesser sentence."

"Pontius would resent my interfering in public," Procula demurred. "I will write a note to him. There is an alcove behind the throne. We will watch from there, and one of the servants can give it to him."

She wrote quickly upon a wax tablet and, calling a soldier, gave orders for it to be given to the procurator immediately, even if the proceedings must be interrupted. Then she guided Joseph and Mary to an alcove near the throne from which they could see the entire room where the hearing was being held.

Pontius Pilate sat upon an elevated dais with the clerks beside him. Flanking them were the lictors, whose upright faces indicated that this was a civil court. The actual proceedings were just beginning, and while they watched, Jesus was brought in, his hands still chained together, between two Roman soldiers. Joseph could see that the Master had been cruelly treated during the night, for his

PILATE WASHING HIS HANDS, Matthias Stom (1600-1650), Musee du Louvre,
Paris, France. © Peter Willi/SuperStock (1158-2577).

face was puffed and bruised, and the marks of scourges were on his body. But the same light shone in his eyes, as if he were seeing something far beyond the vision of those around him, and the same half-smile of pity was upon his lips. After him came the priests led by Caiaphas, his thin-lipped mouth tightly drawn and his eyes cold with hate for the prisoner.

"What charges do you make against this man?" Pilate asked the high priest formally.

"He claims that he is king of the Jews," Caiaphas said, and looked around at the others. "All of us heard him say it."

A chorus of voices concurred with the statement.

"Are you the king of the Jews?" the procurator asked Jesus directly.

Jesus turned to look at him, but for a moment be did not speak. Then he said quietly, "You have said so."

Pilate was obviously taken aback by the answer, and his uncertainty plainly showed on his face. Caiaphas and the others at once broke into a babble of charges against Jesus. . . . As the babble was dying away, the soldier came up to the throne and handed him the wax tablet upon which Claudia Procula had written. Pilate glanced at it quickly, and a startled look came over his face before he turned and looked into the alcove. Seeing his wife standing there, pleading with him wordlessly to have mercy, he seemed to waver for a moment. . . .

Pilate turned to Jesus again and asked,

"See how many charges they bring against you? Have you no answer to make?"

The prisoner did not answer, and the procurator frowned and looked at Caiaphas, as if for advice. Something in the high priest's eyes, perhaps his contempt for the Roman's uncertainty, seemed to sting Pilate, and a faint flush rose in his sallow checks. Then his face hardened and he straightened his shoulders and drew himself more erect, as if he had come to a decision.

"Pontius! No," Claudia Procula cried in a broken voice. But just then a man shouted from the crowd, "Release to us a prisoner as is the custom on this day." The sound of her plea was drowned out by hundreds of voices that took up the cry, demanding that the Roman governor observe the custom of the Passover, when traditionally he released whomever the crowd demanded from prison.

Pilate's face cleared. Here was a way out of the difficulty, for if the crowd demanded the release of Jesus, he would have good reason to grant them the request. "Do you want me to release to you the king of the Jews?" be asked.

Now the final working out of Caiaphas' plan showed itself. For the high priest knew his co-conspirator and his weakness and had cleverly prepared against it. From the front row of the crowd a group of the Temple hangers-on shouted, "No! No! Release to us the man called Barabbas."

And when they had bound him, they led him away, and delivered him to Pontius Pilate the governor. Pilate saith unto them, What shall I do then with Jesus which is called Christ? They all say unto him, Let him be crucified. And the governor said, Why, what evil hath he done? But they cried out the more, saying, Let him be crucified. When Pilate saw that he could prevail nothing, but that rather a tumult was made, he took water, and washed his hands before the multitude, saying, I am innocent of the blood of this just person: see ye to it (MATTHEW 27:2, 22–24).

PONTIUS PILATE

Pilate was detested by the Jews because he was particularly insensitive to their religious convictions. They were angered when Pilate took money from the Temple treasury to build the aqueduct that supplied water to Jerusalem. This act caused a rebellion and Pilate sent his soldiers in and killed many Jews in this rebellion. This may be the incident, or other similar incidents, to which Luke refers in Luke 13:1.

We know little about Pilate but Herod Agrippa I described Pilate in a letter to the emperor Caligula, calling him "naturally inflexible, a blend of self-will and relentlessness." The historian Josephus relates that in A.D. 26, Tiberius appointed Pilate procurator of Judea. There are few facts, but most scholars believe that Pilate was probably a Roman citizen from what we would call the upper-middle class. He lived with his wife, Claudia Procula (Matthew 27:19), in Caesarea, the provincial headquarters. As procurator he had absolute authority over the non-Roman citizens of the province and was responsible to the Roman governor who lodged in Syria. Josephus tells of an incident in which Pilate overran the Samaritans with the result that a complaint against Pilate was filed with his superior, Vitellius, the governor of Syria. Vitellius deposed Pilate and ordered him to stand before the emperor in Rome to answer for his conduct. No more is known of Pontius Pilate.

ECCE HOMO, James J. Tissot (1836-1902). © SuperStock (999-375).

MEMOIRS OF PONTIUS PILATE

JAMES R. MILLS

I saw an old woman who was obviously the carpenter's mother kneeling at the foot of his cross. She was weeping bitterly, and I found myself wondering if she was sorry then for telling him all those stories about the star and the angels.

At noon I ordered an officer to stay all afternoon and report to me whatever he observed. Then I left Calvary and went back into the city; I could not spend the whole day watching those men die. There were a number of other things that required my attention that afternoon.

Soon after I returned to my chamber in the fortress, I noticed through my narrow windows that the sky outside was growing darker. I looked out over the city. It appeared that night was falling long before it should. I saw men and women running up and down the street. Many were screaming or weeping or calling out to their god to save them. It seemed to the Jews to be some sort of super-natural phenomenon. The Christians still feel that way about it, for obvious reasons.

I sent for a horn lantern. When a soldier appeared with one, I walked with him all around the fortress to direct the officers to flog any man who did not exercise proper self-control, and to do it at once. It turned out to be necessary to do that to two or three, but that punishment had the desired effect upon the others, who went about their duties silently.

Thallus the Samaritan, who is certainly a reputable historian, says the darkness at the time of the death of Jesus was the solar eclipse of thirty years ago. All historians are mistaken at times, and he is mistaken in this. The lowering of the sky was a general gloom. It deepened steadily for about an hour until the light of day was extinguished. After another hour that blackness began to disperse very gradually. From beginning to end it lasted three hours. It was an odd sort of atmospheric manifestation.

As night was falling on Jerusalem, I was back in my chamber in the fortress, and I was dictating some officials.

The earthquake was another incident made gravid with meaning by certain scriptures of the Jews. The Christians now quote what seems to be a relevant passage from a Jewish prophet on the subject of the crucifixion of Jesus: "In my distress I called upon the Lord, and cried unto my God. He heard my voice out of his temple, and my cry came to him. Then the earth shook and trembled. The foundations of the hills moved and were shaken."

Later in the afternoon word spread

throughout the city that the earthquake had rent the veil that concealed the most holy place in the Temple. This report also caused dismay among the Jews, and it was soon given symbolic meaning by the Christians. They say it implies that the death of Jesus opened the way to their god.

The religious hierarchy of the Jews did not want to have those three men hanging on their crosses on the Sabbath, which was about to begin, since their days start at sundown rather than at sunrise. Therefore they sent a request that I order the centurion at Calvary to have the men's legs broken to make them die quickly. . . .

"I'll make sure the king of the Jews is really dead," another soldier said, and he thrust a spear into the carpenter's left side.

The carpenter was indeed dead. His hanging body did not react in any way to that wound, although it did leak a lot of blood and lymph. The commentaries of the three astrologers about the star, the stories of Mary and

Joseph about the angels, and those remarks of John the Baptist about his being the Lamb of God had brought the poor fellow to an ignominious end.

PILATE DELIVERING CHRIST TO THE PEOPLE, Christen Dalsgaard (1824-1907), © SuperStock (900-7305).

SIMON OF CYRENE

PAM KENNEDY

It was early in the morning when Simon left the home of his friends and bid goodbye to his sons, Rufus and Alexander. He was determined to get to Jerusalem early and discover for himself the truth about the young teacher so many claimed to be the Messiah. Normally, Simon would not be concerned with such a man, but he felt compelled to examine this itinerant preacher because of the interest of his sons.

For years Simon had instructed his two young sons in the traditions of the Jewish law. Early in the year, he and the two boys, young men now, had set out on the long journey from their Cyrenian home on the North African coast. They traveled along the southern shores of the Mediterranean, through the northern reaches of Egypt, up into the land of Judea, to the city of Jerusalem. They had made arrangements to stay with an old family friend who had land in the countryside.

Soon after their arrival, Alexander and Rufus became fascinated with the teachings of a young Jew named Jesus. Every day they sought out other followers of this teacher and trailed along after them wherever they went. It was nothing to be bothered with, Simon had thought, until they began to bring home tales of miraculous healings, of thousands fed from meager supplies, and even of dead men coming back to life. It was this last claim that had convinced Simon to seek out Jesus himself and put an end to the foolish rumors his sons kept carrying home. He had brought them to Jerusalem to partake in their faith and heritage, not to be led astray by some heretic.

Nearing the gate of the city, Simon stepped to the side of the road to let the jostling crowds pass. There was an unusual number of people hurrying out of the gate for this time of day, he thought. Then, through the clamor of the crowd, Simon heard the unmistakable sound of soldiers marching in cadence, leather and steel creaking and clashing. Dust rising in the hot air glistened in the sun. Then a sound like mourning reached Simon—loud moaning and murmuring as dozens of voices blended together in one sad wail. Simon pushed back to the road's edge to get a better view.

> And they compel one Simon a Cyrenian, who passed by, coming out of the country, the father of Alexander and Rufus, to bear his cross (MARK 15:21).

SIMON OF CYRENE AND HIS TWO SONS, James J. Tissot (1836-1902). © SuperStock (999-9282).

THE VIA DOLOROSA, Jerusalem, Israel. © R. Kord/H. Armstrong Roberts (KR-111850-j).

As he watched the approaching procession, Simon noticed two Roman officers studying him. Suddenly, they left their fellows and strode purposefully toward Simon. The one on the right pulled his flat sword from its scabbard and laid it heavily upon Simon's shoulder. His mouth went dry and his heart pounded in his ears. Although he was from Cyrene, he knew the implication of the soldier's gesture. In Roman occupied Jerusalem, an officer of the occupying forces had only to tap a Jew on the shoulder in order to compel him to perform the most menial or degrading of tasks. The Jew had no choice other than death if he refused to comply.

Yanking him roughly by the cloak, the officer pulled Simon to the center of the dusty road. "Pick up the cross and carry it for this weakling," the Roman snarled as he pushed Simon to the dust next to a dirty, bleeding man. Faced with no alternative, Simon hastened to lift the heavy beam from the shoulders of the criminal. As he did so, the beaten man raised himself to his knees, then struggled to his feet. He stood before Simon, looking into his eyes, and for Simon the look was like a searing flame which burned his very soul. Time and noise and all else seemed to cease and there was only the man and his eyes in all the world. Through his dry lips, Simon managed a hoarse whisper, "Who are you?" and the man answered in a voice that spoke more to Simon's heart than to his ears. "I am Jesus."

In that instant it was as if all his questions were answered, not with words, but with understanding.

Simon turned and began the long climb up the hill named Golgotha, bearing the cross upon which Jesus would soon be crucified. His heart ached with every step as Simon began to see what his sons had come to understand. The words of the prophet Isaiah echoed in his memory: "he was wounded for our transgressions, he was bruised for our iniquities: the chastisement of our peace was upon him; and with his stripes we are healed" (53:5).

Simon turned his head and glanced backward at the stumbling Messiah. Daring the Roman guard's lash, he called in a barely audible whisper, "Is it you, Lord? Are you the long awaited one?"

Jesus raised his head and captured Simon's eyes with his own once more. Exhaustion and pain were there, but something even more compelling than these—pity and love. Slowly, almost imperceptibly, he nodded in reply. Simon's heart leapt. It was true then. All the prophecies were to be fulfilled. Yes, there was tragedy and sorrow at the cross, but the plan of Jehovah would not be thwarted. All the promises would be realized. Simon had not known how God would work, but he had a faith greater than his sight—and a God he knew to be far greater than death.

Man of Cyrene

Avin Harry Johnston

You! You there, without a shirt! You look strong!" The soldier near Simon caught him by the arm and pulled. Simon's arm twisted and jerked. The soldier spun around as if he had been struck a blow.

"Take your hands off me!" Simon's voice was low and hard. His lips had barely moved but his voice cut through the murmur of the crowd clearly. "I'm no slave to Roman commands. I am a free citizen of Cyrene and bow to no man."

The soldier lifted his spear as if to strike. The centurion shouted. The soldier lowered the spear, for Simon had moved forward down the open lane in the midst of the crowd, his feet carrying him of their own accord, it seemed.

His eyes had met those of the man standing beside the fallen cross. He looked into kind eyes, tired eyes, eyes marred with pain. Simon felt a shock equal to a physical blow. Slowly his tightened muscles relaxed. The gaze of the two men remained locked. Although the crowd throbbed and murmured and some even shouted, Simon barely heard them.

As if moved by some invisible force, silent and yet powerful, Simon slowly walked forward.

The soldier lowered his arm and stepped back. The centurion also moved back a step

out of Simon's way. Not a word was spoken aloud. Now even the murmuring of the crowd seemed to subside until it was a mere hum. . . .

Wonderingly, almost in a trance, Simon bent and grasped the cross. He lifted it to his shoulder with one swing. It felt light to him as his whipcord muscles rippled to their duty.

There was a low murmur from those around him at the ease with which he shouldered the wooden beams.

Turning, the man of Cyrene stepped forward with swift and sure stride. No one told him which direction to take. His feet followed an invisible trail down the rough street, into another one, across a square, and into another street. Ahead of him ran men, women, and children. He was dimly aware that a great crowd followed, but he did not look back.

As easily and as carefully as he would have carried a child, Simon bore the cross. He was not conscious of the fact that the wood dug into his bare shoulder, or that the cross arm bumped his knee at every step. Weaker men would have shifted the load. Simon bore it on only one shoulder.

A great peace had settled on him. His heart still throbbed with the suffocating surge, but it was not from the weight of the cross, it was from an inward feeling of something he

JESUS WITH THE CROSS, Titian (Tiziano Vecelli) (1477/89-1576). © SuperStock. (900-196).

could not describe.

Now he understood the meaning of that urge driving him from his boyhood through young manhood into man's estate.

He understood across the years and across the miles from Cyrene that this was the duty he was to perform.

Over uneven stones, past doorways, beneath overhanging eaves the man of Cyrene strode silently, the cross swung clear of the ground, seeming to drift over the heads of those nearby.

Through the streets where people knelt and whispered prayers, where others stood to one side and watched as if attending a feast-day parade, the Cyrenian strode. Not once did he lower his hands from the cross balanced on his bare shoulder.

The feeling of peace and understanding clung to him like a warm mantle. He felt his cheeks wet and understood that they were tears from his own eyes, but he had no conscious impression of crying. One thought only burned deep inside him! He must carry this cross and not let it touch the ground until he would lower to the ground the wooden beams he had taken up for the one who could no longer carry it. In his heart he knew that when he reached the place he was to lower the cross—he would know!

The feeling of contentment welled up within him again. For this he had been born, for this he had lived, and for this he would die, if need be. Simon knew not the name of the bloodmarked man behind him. He knew only that the voice he had heard so many years ago had come again to his ears with the same message.

All this Simon sensed in that brief flash when he had looked deep into the painridden eyes of the man who head bore the thorny crown.

Outside the walls of the city Simon's feet led him to a place where, without a word, he lowered the cross to the ground and stepped back.

The crowd circled him and others as they arrived. Simon turned toward the ones who had just arrived. For another brief moment his eyes again encountered those of the man with the thorn-torn brow. There was a smile in those eyes now, Simon saw.

Again the man of Cyrene was aware of a voice in his ears. "Thank you, my son," the voice seemed to say. "You have done well. That is all you can do."

The centurion stepped between them. Silently and numbly, Simon turned and walked towards the wall of the city.

He did not look back.

It was some time later when he realized he was astride his horse, outside the gates of Jerusalem, and on the open road.

And as they led him away, they laid hold upon one Simon, a Cyrenian, coming out of the country, and on him they laid the cross, that he might bear it after Jesus (LUKE 23:26).

SIMON OF CYRENE

And they compel one Simon a Cyrenian, who passed by, coming out of the country, the father of Alexander and Rufus, to bear his cross (MARK 15:21).

Little is know of Simon of Cyrene who was drafted by the Roman soldiers to carry the cross of Jesus. Simon was described as a man from the country, but he was probably a Jewish pilgrim who had come to Jerusalem for the Passover. Mark identifies Simon as "the father of Alexander and Rufus." The mention of these sons might indicate that they were well known in the Christian community at the time of the Gospel's writing. Paul, in his Epistle to the Romans (Romans 16:13) sends greetings to Rufus, suggesting that the Apostle Paul was close to Rufus. Some scholars believe that Simon of Cyrene was the same person as Simeon called Niger who taught in the church at Antioch. This identification gave rise to the belief that Simon of Cyrene was a black man.

OLIVE TREES IN GARDEN OF GETHSEMANE, JERUSALEM, ISRAEL.
© R. Kord/H. Armstrong Roberts (KR-113269).

THE REPENTANT THIEF
THE REPENTANT THIEF

FULTON OURSLER

The slowly darkening indigo sky was losing its deep violet blue and turning to black. The agony of the gentle prisoner, the memory of his good works, and the wailing of the women all helped to change the mood of the watchers. The compassion of the suffering man moved the people to a dangerous sympathy, so back came the priests with their troupe and they began to jape: "He saved others; let him save himself if he be Christ, the elect of God."

They waggled their hands and fleered and blasphemed. "Wah!" they cried with frenzy. "You that will destroy the Temple of God and in three days build it up again. Wah! Save yourself! Come down from the cross!"

And even Caiaphas, standing with the silent Annas and some of their cronies of the Temple priesthood, spoke out of the side of his mouth: "Others he saved; himself he cannot save."

One of the scribes answered: "If he be the King of Israel let him now come down from the cross and we will believe him."

But there were some who noticed that, as the darkness deepened, a small light shone behind his head, and it grew more luminous as death came ever nearer. . . .

One of the robbers, Gestas, took up the cry from the onlookers and spat it out with blood and foam at his mouth: "If you be the Christ, save yourself—and us!"

But Dysmas, on the right-hand cross, called back to him: "Neither do you fear God, seeing that you are under the same condemnation? And we, indeed, justly—because we receive the due reward of our deeds. But this man has done no evil."

Then, turning his head toward the Master, he said with pleading sweetness, amazing in so rough a voice: "Lord, remember me when you come into your kingdom.

The eyelids of Jesus flew up and he smiled . . . but he called out boldly, in his old clear, strong voice: "So be it, I say to you—this day you shall be with me in Paradise."

> And one of the malefactors which were hanged railed on him, saying, If thou be Christ, save thyself and us. But the other answering rebuked him, saying, . . . we receive the due reward of our deeds: but this man hath done nothing amiss. And he said unto Jesus, Lord, remember me when thou comest into thy kingdom. And Jesus said unto him, Verily I say unto thee, Today shalt thou be with me in paradise (LUKE 23:39–40, 41–43).

Pardoning of the Penitent Thief, James J. Tissot (1836-1902), © SuperStock (999-377).

THE SOLDIERS
AT THE CROSS
AND THEY CAST LOTS

LLOYD C. DOUGLAS

There was not as large a crowd as he had expected to see. There was no disorder, probably because the legionaires were scattered about among the people. It was apparent, from the negligence of the soldiers' posture, as they stood leaning on their lances, that nothing had occurred or was anticipated.

Demetrius moved closer in and joined the outer rim of spectators. Not many of the well-to-do, who had been conspicuous at the Insula, were present. Most of the civilians were poorly dressed. Many of them were weeping. There were several women, heavily veiled and huddled in little groups, in attitudes of silent, hopeless grief. A large circle had been left unoccupied below the crosses.

Edging his way slowly forward, occasionally rising on tiptoe to search for his master, Demetrius paused beside one of the legionaries who, recognizing him with a brief nod, replied to his low-voiced inquiry. The commander and several other officers were on the other side of the knoll, at the rear of the crosses, he said.

"I brought him some water," explained Demetrius, holding up the jug. The soldier showed how many of his teeth were missing.

"That's good," he said. "He can wash his hands. They're not drinking water today. The procurator sent out a wineskin."

"Is the man dead?" asked Demetrius.

"No, he said something awhile ago."

"What did he say? Could you hear?"

"Said he was thirsty."

"Did they give him water?"

"No, they filled a sponge with vinegar that had some sort of balm in it, and raised it to his mouth; but he wouldn't have it. I don't rightly understand what he is up there for, but he's no coward."

The legionaire shifted his position, pointed to the darkening sky, remarked that there was going to be a storm, and moved on through the crowd.

Demetrius did not

> Then the soldiers, when they had crucified Jesus, took his garments, and made four parts, to every soldier a part; and also his coat: now the coat was without seam, woven from the top throughout. They said therefore among themselves, Let us not rend it, but cast lots for it, whose it shall be: that the scripture might be fulfilled, which saith, They parted my raiment among them, and for my vesture they did cast lots. These things therefore the soldiers did (JOHN 19:23–24).

THEY PARTED HIS RAIMENT AND CAST LOTS, James J. Tissot (1836–1902), SuperStock (999-9297).

look at the lonely man again. He edged out into the open and made a wide detour around to the other side of the knoll. Marcellus, Paulus, and four or five others were lounging in a small circle on the ground. A leather dice cup was being shaken negligently, and passed from hand to hand. At first sight of it, Demetrius was hotly indignant. It wasn't like Marcellus to be so brutally unfeeling. A decent man would have to be very drunk indeed to exhibit such callous unconcern in this circumstance.

Now that he was here, Demetrius thought he should inquire whether there was anything he could do for his master. He slowly approached the group of preoccupied officers. After a while, Marcellus glanced up dully and beckoned to him. The others gave him a brief glance and resumed their play.

"Anything you want to tell me?" asked Marcellus, thickly.

"I brought you some water, sir."

"Very good. Put it down there. I'll have a drink presently." It was his turn to play. He shook the cup languidly and tossed out the dice.

"Your lucky day!" growled Paulus. "That finishes me."

He stretched his long arms and laced his fingers behind his head. "Demetrius," he said, nodding toward a rumpled brown mantle that lay near the foot of the central cross, "hand me that coat. I want to look at it."

Demetrius picked up the garment and gave it to him. Paulus examined it with idle interest.

"Not a bad robe," he remarked, holding it up at arm's length. "Woven in the country; dyed with walnut juice. He'll not be needing it anymore. I think I'll say it's mine. How about it, Tribune?"

"Why should it be yours?" asked Marcellus, indifferently. "If it's worth anything, let us toss for it." He handed Paulus the dice cup. "High number wins. It's your turn."

There was a low mutter of thunder in the north and a savage tongue of flame leaped through the black cloud. Paulus tossed a pair of threes, and stared apprehensively at the sky.

"Not hard to beat," said Vinitius, who sat next him. He took the cup and poured out a five and a four. The cup made the circle without bettering this cast until it arrived at Marcellus.

"Double six!" he called. "Demetrius, you take care of the robe. Paulus handed over the garment.

THE CENTURION, James J. Tissot (1836–1902), © SuperStock (999-9310).

FROM THE SIXTH TO THE NINTH HOUR

LLOYD C. DOUGLAS

Rebuke these people!" he shouted, angrily. "They are saying that the storm is a judgment on us!" . . .

There was another gigantic crash of thunder.

"Maybe it is!" yelled Marcellus, recklessly.

The fat man waved a menacing fist.

"It is your duty to keep order here!" he shrieked.

"Do you want me to stop the storm?" demanded Marcellus.

"Stop the blasphemy! These people are crying out that this Galilean is the Son of God!"

"Maybe he is!" shouted Marcellus. "You wouldn't know!" He was fumbling with the hilt of his sword. The fat man backed away, howling that the procurator should hear of this.

Circling the knoll, Demetrius paused for a final look at the lonely man on the central cross. He had raised his face and was gazing up into the black sky. Suddenly he burst forth with a resonant call, as if crying to a distant friend for aid.

A poorly dressed bearded man of middle age, apparently one of the Galilean's friends from the country, rushed out of the crowd and ran down the slope weeping aloud in an abandon of grief. Demetrius grasped him by the sleeve as he stumbled past.

"What did he say?"

The man made no reply, tore himself loose, and ran on shouting his unintelligible lamentations.

Now the dying Galilean was looking down upon the crowd below him. His lips moved. His eyes surveyed the people with the same sorrow they had expressed on the road when the multitude had hailed him as their king. There was another savage burst of thunder. The darkness deepened.

Demetrius rolled up the robe and thrust it inside his tunic, pressing it tightly under his arm. The intimate touch of the garment relieved his feeling of desolation. He wondered if Marcellus might let him keep the robe. It would be a

> And it was about the sixth hour, and there was a darkness over all the earth until the ninth hour. And the sun was darkened, and the veil of the temple was rent in the midst. And when Jesus had cried with a loud voice, he said, Father, into thy hands I commend my spirit: and having said thus, he gave up the ghost (LUKE 23:44—46).

THE EARTHQUAKE, James J. Tissot (1836–1902). © SuperStock (999–50).

comfort to own something that this coura-geous man had worn. He would cherish it as a priceless inheritance. It would have been a great experience, he felt, to have known this man—to have learned the nature of his mind. Now that there would be no opportunity to share his friendship, it would be an enduring consolation to possess his robe.

Turning about, with swimming eyes, he started down the hill. It was growing so dark now that the narrow path was indistinct. He flung a backward look over his shoulder, but the descending gloom had swallowed up the knoll.

By the time he reached the city streets, night had fallen on Jerusalem, though it was only mid-afternoon. Lights flickered in the windows. Pedestrians moved slowly, carrying torches. Frightened voices called to one another. Demetrius could not understand what they were saying, but their tone was apprehensive, as if they were wondering about the cause of this strange darkness. He wondered, too, but felt no sense of depression or alarm. The sensation of being alone and unwanted in an unfriendly world had left him. He was not lonely now. He hugged the robe close to his side as if it contained some inexpli-cable remedy for heartache.

Melas was standing in the corridor, in front of Paulus's door, when he arrived at the barracks. Demetrius was in no mood to talk, and proceeded to his master's quarters, Melas following with his torch.

"So, you went out there, eh?" said the Thracian, grimly. "How did you like it?" They entered the room and Melas applied his torch to the big stone lamps. Receiving no answer to his rough query, he asked, "What do you think this is; an eclipse?"

"I don't know," replied Demetrius, "Never heard of an eclipse lasting so long."

"Maybe it's the end of the world," said Melas, forcing an uncouth laugh.

"That will be all right with me," said Demetrius.

"Think this Jesus has had anything to do with it?" asked Melas, half in earnest.

"No," said Demetrius, "I shouldn't think so."

Melas sauntered toward the door. Demetrius, thinking he had gone, drew out the robe and unfolded it under the light.

"What have you there?" queried Melas, from the doorway.

"His robe," said Demetrius.

Melas came back and regarded the blood-stained garment with silent interest.

"How do you happen to have it?" he asked, in an awed tone.

"It belongs to the legate. The officers tossed for it. He won it."

"I shouldn't think he'd want it,"

remarked Melas. "I'm sure I wouldn't. It will probably bring him bad luck."

GOLGOTHA, JERUSALEM, ISRAEL. © R. Opfer/H. Armstrong Roberts (KR-63509).

"Why bad luck?" demanded Demetrius.

"It belonged to a brave man."

THE CENTURION'S STORY

PAM KENNEDY

It was a hot, dusty day in Jerusalem, and Marcus was in an ill humor. He had been summoned to supervise a crucifixion. This was an unusual duty for a centurion, but Pilate, the Roman governor of occupied Judea, was nervous about this particular crucifixion. Consequently, Marcus, who regularly commanded a company of one hundred men, had been ordered to lead the small contingent of soldiers tasked with the execution.

There were three men to be crucified today: two were thieves and one was a religious zealot of some sort. Apparently Pilate had sentenced this third man because of complaints brought by the Jewish leaders. Marcus cared little about the particulars of the case. His interest was in doing his duty to the satisfaction of his superiors.

As the small party of soldiers and condemned men began the death march to Golgotha, Marcus's attention was riveted upon the one called Jesus. It was obvious the man had been brutalized, beaten with a scourge and seriously injured. He staggered under the weight of the wooden crossbeam he carried, stumbled, and nearly fell. Partly in mercy, but more for expediency, Marcus compelled a bystander to lift the beam and carry it the distance to the hill outside the city gates.

It was at that point Marcus first con-

Now from the sixth hour there was darkness over all the land unto the ninth hour. And about the ninth hour Jesus cried with a loud voice, saying, Eli, Eli, lama sabachthani? that is to say, My God, my God, why hast thou forsaken me? Some of them that stood there, when they heard that, said, This man calleth for Elias. And straightway one of them ran, and took a sponge, and filled it with vinegar, and put it on a reed, and gave him to drink. The rest said, Let be, let us see whether Elias will come to save him. Jesus, when he had cried again with a loud voice, yielded up the ghost. And, behold, the veil of the temple was rent in twain from the top to the bottom; and the earth did quake, and the rocks rent; And the graves were opened; and many bodies of the saints which slept arose, And came out of the graves after his resurrection, and went into the holy city, and appeared unto many. Now when the centurion, and they that were with him, watching Jesus, saw the earthquake, and those things that were done, they feared greatly, saying, Truly this was the Son of God (MATTHEW 27:45–54).

fronted Jesus face-to-face, for as the weight was taken from his back, the wounded man straightened and captured the eyes of the centurion with his own. It was a most unsettling look and Marcus quickly turned aside. Pity? Mourning? Grief? The centurion couldn't put a name to it. He had seen many men face death with eyes of anger, hatred, or fear; but none of that was present in this man. Marcus wondered why.

The hill was gained, the men were hung upon the crosses, and Marcus watched with disdain as the soldiers joked and cast lots for the condemned men's cast-off clothes. The centurion stood apart observing the scene as he would a play. He noticed things that had not previously caught his attention. Small groups of women huddled in prayer, weeping silently. Groups of passersby, priests, and city rulers taunted the one called Jesus, challenging him to come down, to prove his claims of deity.

Watching it all, Marcus recalled the stories he had heard over the past three years. Stories of a healer, a teacher, a rabbi who had roamed the countryside speaking about the kingdom of God. He recalled a fellow centurion's story of how this man had healed a dying slave—without ever seeing the man. Marcus remembered now and studied this man called Jesus.

For three long hours he watched. There was no railing at the frenzied crowd or the greedy soldiers, no curses directed at God or man. Instead, to the centurion's surprise, he heard Jesus speak words of forgiveness, of comfort, of encouragement. Almost unconsciously, Marcus moved closer to the cross. Whether it was to hear Jesus' words better or from some other more supernatural compulsion, he didn't know. But in the end, Marcus stood nearly below the crucified man, his eyes captured once again by those of Jesus.

Then the darkness came, chill and black and heavy as a shroud. It was noon, but as dark as midnight—without stars or moon. Still Marcus stood transfixed, outside of time, it seemed, staring at the outstretched arms, the lolling head, the bleeding brow.

Finally the wounded head raised, the eyes opened, the chest heaved with the intake of air and a cry shattered the blackness.

"My God, my God! Why hast thou forsaken me?"

Marcus started as Jesus shouted to eternity, and brightness pierced the dark. His heart racing, the centurion ordered the soldiers to raise a vinegar-soaked sponge to the condemned man's lips.

"Speak!" Marcus cried, something in him screaming for confirmation of the truth he suspected, for a moment of clear illumination. Was this man truly who he claimed to be? Marcus needed some kind of proof for what his mind and heart were stretching to comprehend.

And then the cry resounded over the bleak hillside. "It is finished!" It was the victor's cry, shouted by the winner of a race, the

one triumphant over his enemies in battle. It was the confirmation Marcus sought!

Falling to his knees before the rugged cross, Marcus heard Jesus speak once more, this time in tones of confidence and peace.

"Father, into thy hands I commend my spirit."

Marcus watched as the body slumped, lifeless, on the cross. This was no execution, but a confident, deliberate yielding of life.

As if wrenched in terrestrial grief, the earth beneath Marcus's knees trembled and groaned. Rocks split in deafening cracks. Men and women screamed, ran, and were thrown to the convulsing ground. But for Marcus, fear had passed. He had been lifted by this man called Jesus to a place beyond terror.

His eyes burning with unshed tears, his mind gripping the truth at last, Marcus raised his arms in supplication and praise. There on Golgotha, giving voice to the thunder, the centurion cried out to heaven, "Truly this man was the Son of God!"

THE CENTURION GLORIFIES GOD, James J. Tissot (1836–1902). © SuperStock (999-9309).

THE FAITH OF THE CENTURION

Edwin McNeill Poteat

The centurion was scrupulous to a fault in the performance of his duty, and he was irritated by what he thought was an unnecessary delay outside the gate as they were on their way to Skull Hill. The Galilean stumbled and fell, but his fall was broken by a man who caught the cross as it slipped from his shoulder. That a spectator should help a felon was strange enough, but it was stranger that a felon would allow it. It was a part of the code to scorn every show of pity, and to accept help was a confession of weakness; but this man asked, with a show of deep solicitude, if his benefactor felt the cross too heavy for him. As was the custom, women cried out in accusation or in pity as their sympathies dictated, but instead of the lewd retort that was customarily heard, this man spoke with tender pity to those who were bereft of kin or burdened with loneliness. A hush like a sudden lull in a storm had followed his words, and faces showed a respite from anguish, and the centurion himself felt the strange pervasive lessening of tension. It was a full minute before he shook off the spell and called the cavalcade to order and to march. For the first time he found it hard to watch the brutal job of driving the nails through a man's hands. He offered no resistance to the executioners, in striking contrast to the writhing struggles of the thieves on either side of him. An hour later when the young legionary who, at his scourging in the morning had kept the score for the scourge master, took a flask of drugged wine from a bystander and offered him a drink to dull his pain and ease the torture of dying, he declined it. This, Domitius realized later, was neither stubbornness nor bravado. The man who had made no truce with life was asking no truce with death; he who had seen clearly into the heart of humanity was loath to look into the face of God with his brain fogged by an anodyne. Into the mind of Domitius flashed pictures of the drunken orgies of those who boasted in Rome their lordship over life and laid claims to divinity, but who took flight from their own bitterness and disillusion in a draft of nepenthe or by the sting of an asp.

After this, Jesus knowing that all things were now accomplished, that the scripture might be fulfilled, saith, I thirst. Now there was set a vessel full of vinegar: and they filled a sponge with vinegar, and put it upon hyssop, and put it to his mouth. When Jesus therefore had received the vinegar, he said, It is finished: and he bowed his head, and gave up the ghost (JOHN 19: 28–30).

The taunts of the mob evoked no reply from him. He silenced the thieves who hung beside him with a quiet word. To his mother, trembling nearby on the arm of a friend he spoke reassuringly, and then he prayed—not to an image in a gaudy shrine, and not with a bleeding victim freshly slain, nor with an offering for a venal priest. For those who had judged him falsely, condemned him unjustly, and slain him cruelly, he asked forgiveness, and then with a sigh that marked an epoch in the history of the world, he acknowledged the realization of his eternal destiny, and committed his soul to his Father. Here was spiritual fortitude and confidence as inexplicable as his physical courage, but that was the end of him. Or was it?

A tremor rippled beneath the surface of the earth, shuddered up and over the hill and was gone. The sky above the summit, seemed to spiral upward in a black vortex and then dip in a golden whorl to the earth as if to salute the dying with a portent of heaven. The crowd on the hilltop suddenly stopped their taunting cries, lifted their faces, white with terror, to the sky, and departed silently for the city, beating their breasts. The soldiers gave up their dicing at the foot of the cross.

Domitius dropped to his knees and bowed his head in reverent wonder. Through his mind trooped a succession of figures, resplendent with the glories of the earth: Jupiter, Janus and Vesta, Cybele, Bacchus and Mithra, and last of all Julius and Augustus. He opened his eyes. The crowd was gone. A shaft of golden light broke like a flying javelin from the phalanx of dark cloud that crowded the west, and for a transforming interval illumined the center cross with a soft ethereal glow. Domitius got slowly to his feet and lifted his eyes toward the face, now passionless in death. He remembered a promise made before the door of a rude hut, many years ago, and with a sensation of fulfillment he was never able to explain said: "Truly this was the Son of God."

CONFESSIONS OF LONGIN, James J. Tissot (1836–1902). © SuperStock 999-9316).

A BOND IS FORMED

BERTHA M. PETERSON

Gaius and his men had returned to Antonia, tired from a hard day's work this time. Going to his apartment after making his final report to his superior officer, he suddenly felt like an old man. Centuries seemed to have passed over his head since he had gone on duty that morning, and there was a positive change in him. He felt as if he were almost a different person.

That man Jesus, whom they had crucified—Gaius had heard of him, had actually seen him before; but he had been a total stranger. Now it seemed almost as if he were in the very room—not a menacing but a friendly presence, almost beloved. What caused this feeling? Gaius could not say.

Then that lad, Lucius. Suddenly the longing he had felt earlier in the day came to the centurion again. He wished he had a son—a boy like this Lucius, for instance. But some Sabine shepherd was boasting to his neighbors of his soldier son, rejoicing in the possession of stalwart offspring. The boy belonged to someone else, not to him.

And yet—there had been something between them out there on Calvary, something more than the

Then said Jesus, Father, forgive them; for they know not what they do. And they parted his raiment, and cast lots (LUKE 23:34).

relationship between officer and man. Of all his soldiers, Lucius was the only one who had perceived any worth in Jesus. Actions noted and recorded in his mind, but pushed back by the quick developments and duties of the day, returned: the other men mocking and taunting; the young soldier silently seated in the deep recess of the window; his overzealousness as guard; the flaunting of discipline in leaving his assigned place; his obstructing Porcius in his duty so as to protect Jesus; his bold suggestion to his superior officer; his offer of reward to the countryman to carry the cross; his resentment of the taunts of his comrades at the cross; his grief at the death of Jesus; his attempt to deflect the spear of Quintus—what did this mean unless, somehow, a bond existed between Lucius and Jesus?

That could also make a bond between Lucius and Gaius himself.

"I shall cultivate that boy as much as discipline allows and overlook his breach of discipline today," thought the centurion, as he ate his simple repast.

Meanwhile, in the guardroom, the returned soldiers drank their wine and ate their coarse food. Contrary to his usual activity as clown of the barracks, Lucius sat apart and silent. He also was recalling certain memories of the day, as had the centurion.

The crowning of Jesus with the thorns, which he had thought very clever at the time—now he would have given his life to have it undone. He could still see the kind eyes, gently reproachful, yet pitying him. Then there was the cry of forgiveness from the cross. Somehow the young Roman did not realize it had been for the crowd, but hugged it to himself. It had brought sweet, peaceful relief from that pain which was not of the body. He would like to know more about Jesus. Perhaps that young man who had taken the mother to his home could tell him. Lucius would watch for him. The priests and the people could not give him what he wanted. That was evident.

Then there was that mother and her great love for her son. Here, too, was a sweetness and purity of which he had been exceedingly ignorant. It suddenly seemed to Lucius as if he had scarcely been living before and that he was now starting anew, learning—in one day— more than in all the other years of his life.

And then—the centurion. That usually stern man had been nearly intimate with the youngest and least experienced of his century. He had been almost like a father. Lucius suddenly realized that he knew as little about fathers as mothers.

Besides, the centurion had shown a faith in Jesus and kindness toward his mother. The cough had not deceived Lucius. He was beginning to suspect what Pilate, the other officers and his comrades had not—that under the brusque, coarse exterior of the man lay a warm heart; and the centurion lost no respect thereby in the eyes of Lucius.

The mind of Lucius went back to the almost fatherly attitude of the centurion. What a father he would make. Lucius would have been proud to own him as such, but the centurion would not even care to adopt him, once he knew the young soldier's origin. At least, so Lucius thought.

But there was somehow a bond between himself and Jesus, the centurion and Jesus and lastly, between the officer and Lucius himself—a bond that did not come only from their association in the century.

"I wish I understood it all," thought the young soldier, puzzled, yet not anxious.

GUARDS AT THE TOMB

GUARD DUTY

PAM KENNEDY

J ason, Marcus, Articus! Come here!" The orders echoed across the garrison's courtyard as the three soldiers hurried to the centurion's side, stood at attention, and saluted.

"These priests from the temple have requested a guard for the tomb of their recently deceased friend."

"He was most certainly not our friend," interrupted one of the rabbis.

"Pilate has graciously granted this unusual request," the centurion continued. "You three are to make certain that thieves do not break into the tomb. That is all."

"Come along," an aging rabbi ordered, and the small party walked quickly through the garrison's gates and along the dusty streets of Jerusalem until they came to a small walled garden. At the garden's far side, shaded by an ancient acacia, was a large tomb, its entrance sealed with a rough stone wheel.

"There it is," announced one of the rabbis. "The body is inside, but we suspect his followers may try to steal

And when they were assembled with the elders, and had taken counsel, they gave large money unto the soldiers, Saying, Say ye, His disciples came by night, and stole him away while we slept. And if this come to the governor's ears, we will persuade him, and secure you. So they took the money, and did as they were taught. (MATTHEW 28:12–15).

it in order to feign a resurrection. It will be your responsibility to see that this does not occur. Do you understand?'

Jason's face flushed with anger at the priest's tone. "I am sure we shall have no difficulty," he replied, "but to ease your minds, we shall place a Roman seal upon the tomb."

Through the night, the guards took their turns on watch. At dawn, Jason stood beside the acacia as a gentle breeze swept through the garden. Suddenly, the wind hushed, the birds became still, and the leaves hung motionless. Jason's pulse began to race, and he dashed to wake the others. "Get up! Hurry! Something very odd is happening."

The earth began to roll and pitch, and the guards staggered, clinging to one another for support. A brilliant light enveloped the garden. Stunned, Articus pointed a trembling finger toward the tomb. "Look!" he gasped.

A man dressed in dazzling white effortlessly pushed the heavy stone away from the tomb's entrance. Then, seating himself upon the stone, he examined the trio of soldiers. Jason's heart pounded and his body shook with terror beneath the angel's gaze. Overcome with fear, the three fell to the ground, unconscious.

Jason was the first to rise. The blinding light was gone, and he heard muffled voices near the open tomb. He edged nearer until he could make out two women conversing with the angel. He held his breath, listening to their words.

The angel comforted them, then said: "Be not affrighted: Ye seek Jesus of Nazareth which was crucified. He is risen. He is not here. Behold the place where they laid him. But go your way, tell his disciples and Peter that he goeth before you into Galilee. There shall ye see him, as he said unto you."

The women looked at the angel with awe and then gripped each other in a joyful embrace. "Go now," the angel urged, and the two women hurried from the garden. The angel turned, and his eyes met Jason's for one piercing moment. Then he was gone, vanished; only the dim light of the early dawn remained.

Jason glanced back at his fellow guards, still unconscious on the ground, then crept slowly to the tomb. Stepping over the broken Roman seal, he entered the crypt. Once inside, he saw the linen clothes lying undisturbed on the bier as if the body had merely evaporated from within them. He recalled the mysterious man's words: "He is risen."

Hastening outside again, Jason ran to Articus and Marcus, who were beginning to stir. "The body is gone," he announced.

"How are we going to explain this?" asked Articus angrily. "The centurion will have our heads for this, mark my words."

Jason thought. "It was the rabbis who insisted upon the guards. I suggest we go to them first. At least we can buy some time."

The three soldiers quickly gathered their gear and ran to the Temple's courtyard. Articus slowly and dramatically told the incredulous rabbi of the earthquake, the rolling back of the stone, and the man dressed in glowing white. When Articus finished, the priest instructed the soldiers to wait while he conferred with his fellow rabbis.

Shortly, the chief priest returned. He handed Jason a leather bag. "Here is a large sum of money. Divide it among yourselves. If you are questioned about your experiences this morning, say this: 'His disciples came by night, and stole him away while we slept.' Now be off and let me never see any of you again."

As they returned to the garrison, the three divided the Roman coins carefully. Articus and Marcus joked about how they would spend their windfall and turned to Jason. "What about you, Jason, what will you buy?" teased Articus.

Testing the weight of the gold, Jason recalled the angel's words, "He is risen!" He remembered the women's joy and their haste to share the news. He regarded his friends for a moment then replied, "I have decided to go to Galilee. There is someone there I need to see."

THE WATCH IS SET

JIM BISHOP

What worried Annas was that the faker Jesus had said, in his teachings, that he would rise again in three days. Now that he was dead, there was one more chore to do. The high priests would have to go to Pontius Pilate in the morning and ask for guards to be posted over the tomb of Joseph of Arimathaea so that the scheming disciples of this man could not come and steal the body and claim later that he had risen from the dead.

So when his son-in-law and the others had concluded their horrifying story of dishonor, Annas wet his aged lips and advised them to be more concerned with the promise of Jesus to resurrect himself from the dead. The high priests had not thought of this, and at once they began to babble. Annas shushed them all, and told them to delegate a committee to go to the Gentile at Antonia and, if possible, to have him post a Roman guard over the tomb for several days.

The importance of this was twofold: first, it would have the same effect as having the Romans participate in the original raid on the Gethsemane—once they became a part of it, the Romans would have to protect their interests by not permitting anyone to steal the body; second, the word of the Romans would have more weight with the people of Jerusalem at this time. If the priests said that Jesus did not rise from the grave, the thousands of followers of the Galilean would say that the priests were lying to cover the darkness of their deed in having him crucified; if the Romans said it, the people would believe, understanding that the Gentiles had no interest in the matter one way or the other.

Caiaphas praised his father-in-law as a man of great wisdom.

Now the next day, that followed the day of the preparation, the chief priests and Pharisees came together unto Pilate, Saying, Sir, we remember that that deceiver said, while he was yet alive, After three days I will rise again. Command therefore that the sepulchre be made sure until the third day, lest his disciples come by night, and steal him away, and say unto the people, He is risen from the dead: so the last error shall be worse than the first. Pilate said unto them, Ye have a watch: go your way, make it as sure as ye can. So they went, and made the sepulchre sure, sealing the stone, and setting a watch (MATTHEW 27:62–66).

THE EVIL COUNSEL OF CAIAPHAS, James J. Tissot (1836–1902). © SuperStock (999-187).

NICODEMUS
WHO CAME BY NIGHT

Nicholas Roland

"It is true," said Joseph. "They have done it, exactly as you feared."

Nicodemus, rising from his bed, clothed and in his right mind again, had gone straight to see him, his ally in the affair.

"Then there was no trial?"

"Nothing within the Law. We were not told until it was all over. Azzai, Gamaliel and myself."

"Who did it then?"

"Annas, his men and all the jackals. They held a meeting packed with their own mob, just to give color to the business for the Romans."

"And Samuel?" Nicodemus was sad. Annas had only behaved according to his nature, but Samuel was an angel.

"Samuel knew, but he did nothing. He let things take their course. He said that Annas was protecting the Law by acting outside it."

"Oh Samuel, my friend!" . . .

"If you had been there," said Joseph, "they could not have done it. You would have been watching, and you would have found out."

"But the Romans? They are just."

"Not Pilate. Annas and the jackals threatened him. He held out for a little, but they wore him down. 'You are no friend of Caesar!' Their usual line of attack."

"He must have thought they spoke for all our people," said Nicodemus. "But they did not. I fell ill before I could tell Festus." He wished he had stayed mad, waking to a world of such horror, a horror that seemed to have happened only because he was mad.

"But now," said Joseph, "it is all over. Jesus of Nazareth is dead."

There was safety for the mind only in action. "There are only three hours left to bury him," said Nicodemus. At nightfall it would be Sabbath, and the Passover supper too. "Where are his followers? They should see to it."

"They are scattered. They are like chickens who have lost their mother," said Joseph.

"The ones I know," said Nicodemus,

> And there came also Nicodemus, which at the first came to Jesus by night, and brought a mixture of myrrh and aloes, about an hundred pound weight. Then took they the body of Jesus, and wound it in linen clothes with the spices, as the manner of the Jews is to bury (JOHN 19: 39–40).

"may turn out more than chickens, when they grow up."

"But now they are absolutely useless."

The two men looked at each other, patricians of the House of Israel, equal in spirit though not in guile to Annas, contemptuous of the jackals, fearing their fellows less than they feared another hazard, but this too they overcame.

"We shall not be able to eat the Passover because of corpse defilement," said Nicodemus. "But for this body it is worth it. We could not save him living, but we can bury him now he is dead."

A slave knocked the wedge away, and the stone rolled in its groove downward, closing the entrance to the cave.

The two men stood there for a moment, saluting in memory.

"Jesus is dead," said Nicodemus, "but he will live forever. The men who killed him have made sure of that."

Joseph of Arimathaea looked at him curiously, in the fading evening light. His friend had not really returned to normal. "You are as cheerful," said Joseph, "as if he was your greatest enemy, and you are mourning as if he was your greatest friend."

"I am mourning," said Nicodemus sadly, smiling. "Israel has slain another prophet, and he was also my friend."

How impossible to say more, thought Nicodemus, to tell another prophet had been put to death.

"Is it not strange," said Joseph, "the way you were restored? It almost looks like the last and most extraordinary of the Rabbi's works. But of course it can't be, because he was already dead."

They turned to go back to the city, past the group of women watching and the knoll with the three posts of wood. The eastern sky was not yet bright with the moon's rising but a single star was there. The wall cut off the view of the city and all but the topmost parts of the Temple, but northward in the open there were houses among the gardens. Then with the second and the third stars appearing, there was the sound of trumpets, and the lights in the houses were kindled. The Sabbath had begun to shine.

It was less than ten minutes' walk to the house of Nicodemus. They shivered, for after nightfall it was cold. They were the only people abroad. Nicodemus felt excluded from the world which he inhabited: within the houses the Passover supper was going forward. Until this year, in all his life, he had never missed.

Joseph left in the direction of his own quarters, and Nicodemus entered the house alone. John was waiting: the porter knew him. Somewhere, also, there were two women. "There is no Passover for us today," said Nicodemus. He sent for a maidservant to look after the women.

Nicodemus did not explain himself. John

knew enough, though not everything. He had listened to the evil spirit speaking when Nicodemus first went mad, though he knew nothing of what came after, for Nicodemus never spoke of what had passed when they took him to see Jesus, during his madness.

John saw that his master, having failed to convince Nicodemus in his lifetime that he was merely human, had now succeeded, by dying in the usual way. The recovery of Nicodemus was therefore not surprising. John took up their old relationship where it had left off, but now in greater dependence. His true master had vanished, and only Nicodemus was left.

"There is nothing to be afraid of, my son," said Nicodemus briskly. "Everything will turn out all right."

"We had thought that he would be the one to redeem Israel," said John miserably, weeping: for Jesus, or for himself? He was a boy again.

"So he may," said Nicodemus comfortingly, with more assurance than he felt. "Though not in the way you thought. He was a prophet."

"We looked for his kingdom on earth."

"God has arranged things differently."

"We do not understand."

"You are not the only people. There are things which I too do not understand. He would not have died if I had not been stricken, and I was made well again only by his death."

After a little, Nicodemus continued. He asked about John's plans. Already he saw the future: the life-interest of Rabbi Jesus in his followers having lapsed, John might be going free. A whole lifetime to recall the words of Jesus and to seek their meaning.

"We cannot stay with Azzai, he will be in danger. Tonight we are going to Bethany, we hope."

"Who is 'we'?"

"There is my mother and her sister, who are here already, and my brother and Simon Peter, and three other women."

The first time that John had come to his house, Nicodemus had detained him at the last moment as he was leaving. Nicodemus had felt then that it was a moment of decision, something tremendous for both John and himself. Now he again had this feeling, and he said at once, "Bethany is beyond, a Sabbath day's journey, and also it is dark and you might not get out of the city. You must stay here."

"There are many of us," said John, "and you would be in danger."

"My house is large," said Nicodemus, "and there is no danger, either to you or to me. Annas would not dare."

John was too tired to thank him properly. "In a day or two," he said, "when everything is quiet, we can go home and get back to our fishing."

NICODEMUS, James J. Tissot (1836–1902). © SuperStock (999-9965).

BLIND NICODEMUS. © Sipley/H. Armstrong Roberts (KR-9317).

There was a man of the Pharisees, named Nicodemus, a ruler of the Jews: The same came to Jesus by night, and said unto him, Rabbi, we know that thou art a teacher come from God: for no man can do these miracles that thou doest, except God be with him. Jesus answered and said unto him, Verily, verily, I say unto thee, Except a man be born again, he cannot see the kingdom of God. Nicodemus saith unto him, How can a man be born when he is old? can he enter the second time into his mother's womb, and be born? Jesus answered, Verily, verily, I say unto thee, Except a man be born of water and of the Spirit, he cannot enter into the kingdom of God (JOHN 3:1–5).

NICODEMUS

A Pharisee and member of the Sanhedrin, Nicodemus was probably well trained in Old Testament law and tradition. He was wealthy, educated, and powerful, yet it was to Nicodemus that Jesus said, "Ye must be born again." This is the first time Nicodemus is mentioned in the Bible.

He is mentioned two more times in Scripture. In the Gospel of John, after the Sanhedrin denounces Jesus as a false prophet, Nicodemus is a cautious supporter of Jesus as he counsels caution: "Doth our law judge any man, before it hear him, and know what he doeth" (John 7:51).

But the third and last time Nicodemus's name appears in Scripture, he can be seen as a public supporter of the crucified Christ. Nicodemus comes to the tomb with about a hundred pounds of spices to be placed between the folds of the cloth in which Jesus was buried. No more is known of Nicodemus, but in only three Scripture references, we have seen him hear the truth for the first time, watch him take his first tentative steps in faith, and finally, we watch him unashamedly hurrying to the tomb with a heavy load to leave at the tomb of his crucified Savior.

AN ACT OF COURAGE

JIM BISHOP

It required a degree of courage, indeed gallantry, to do what Joseph of Arimathaea did that afternoon. He hurried to Antonia and requested an audience of Pontius Pilate. It was granted, and Joseph asked for permission to bury Jesus of Nazareth at once.

Pilate was startled. He did not believe that Jesus was yet dead. Joseph insisted that he had seen him die with his own eyes. To settle the matter, the Roman ordered a horseman to Golgotha at once to get a report from Abenadar. Joseph waited. This was an embarrassing interview for him, because in asking for the body for burial, he was making known to the procurator that he, a member of the Sanhedrin, the head of the well-known Sadducean family, was a secret disciple of Jesus.

Why else would he ask for the body? Why would he demean himself by coming to Antonia, when at this moment he should be in the Temple across the courtyard holding a baby lamb as thousands of men were now doing, while they waited the three separate calls to sacrifice? He must have known that it would please the pagan procurator to know that, even in the Sanhedrin, there were secret followers of the Galilean.

He waited. Word came back that the man Jesus had died first, just prior to the work of the guard with the plank. Pilate shrugged. He bowed pleasantly and gave permission for Joseph to take the body down, in conformity with Jewish custom, and to bury the body before the onset of the Sabbath.

The Hebrew senator thanked him and hurried back through the double arch and out into the streets of Jerusalem. There, by accident, he met Nicodemus, the Pharisee who

> Joseph of Arimathaea, an honourable counsellor, which also waited for the kingdom of God, came, and went in boldly unto Pilate, and craved the body of Jesus. And Pilate marvelled if he were already dead: and calling unto him the centurion, he asked him whether he had been any while dead. And when he knew it of the centurion, he gave the body to Joseph. And he bought fine linen, and took him down, and wrapped him in the linen, and laid him in a sepulchre which was hewn out of a rock, and rolled a stone unto the door of the sepulchre (MARK 15:43–46).

THE DESCENT FROM THE CROSS, Rembrandt Harmensz van Rijn (1606-1669),
National Gallery of Art, Washington, D.C. © SuperStock (463-4798).

had once sought Jesus in the dead of night, and Joseph said that he had just built a sepulcher in the garden at Golgotha and was about to inter the body of Jesus there. Nicodemus did not hesitate. He said that he too had been strangely moved by the words and deeds of this man, and he wanted to assist in the funeral arrangements to see that Jesus was buried as an honorable man.

It is an almost melodramatic irony that, when Jesus died, his burial was arranged—not by Peter, or John, or the others who only on the previous night had beat their breasts at dinner and argued about who loved him the most—but by a Sadducee, a Pharisee, and a pagan. The Roman custom was to permit the bodies to remain on the cross until the carrion birds, the dogs and other small animals and insects had had sufficient time to reduce the body to bones. It was Caesar Augustus who broke the custom and gave the Jews permission to take down those who could be certified as dead, and bury them before the Sabbath.

Joseph knew—and so did Nicodemus—that when they reached Golgotha, a few of the priests would still be there, and would be scandalized to learn that two of the most respected men in the land—would publicly lay the blasphemer to rest. Thus, though they had hidden their devotion to the Messiah throughout his life, now they were bringing down on themselves the condemnation of their own kind for the rest of their lives. The elite of Jerusalem could never forgive these men for assisting a scoundrel who had been crucified.

It was Nicodemus who sent a servant to his home for one hundred pounds of spices, a mixture of myrrh and aloes—which was necessary for the final anointment of the body. Joseph purchased wide bands of fine linen to be used as funeral shrouds. He also secured other unguents and a small downy feather.

When they arrived at Golgotha, Joseph and Nicodemus approached the friends of Jesus and told John that the Romans had given the body to the Arimathaean for burial. John searched their faces, and saw love and pity. They discussed the need for haste so that the Sabbath would not be profaned, and Joseph pointed to the proximity of the sepulcher which was newly hewn from rock.

John said that he would help to take the body down. The two men of compassion said no, that John should remain at the side of the mother. They would do this thing, now that the Romans had left. The few high priests who were watching came closer to listen and were shocked to the point of momentary muteness when they saw two of the great Jewish leaders of the Temple with the kin of the blasphemer. And when they understood that Jesus would be buried in Joseph's own crypt, they muttered against their leaders and hurried into Jerusalem to confer with Annas.

JOSEPH OF ARIMATHAEA

> And after this Joseph of Arimathaea, being a disciple of Jesus, but secretly for fear of the Jews, besought Pilate that he might take away the body of Jesus: and Pilate gave him leave. He came therefore, and took the body of Jesus (JOHN 19:38).

Joseph most likely hailed from a town in southern Samaria and was probably living in Jerusalem at the time of the crucifixion. He might have been a dissenting member of the Sanhedrin that had condemned Jesus to death. Joseph is identified by both Matthew and John as a secret disciple of Jesus.

Joseph must have been a man of great wealth and high social standing in order to approach Pontius Pilate directly and ask that Jesus' body be given to him. He was, however, risking his reputation and perhaps his life.

Joseph placed Jesus' body in a new tomb which might have been one Joseph had obtained for his family's use. Scripture does not mention any of Jesus' apostles being present at the burial. This was left to Joseph, Nicodemus, and the women. No more is revealed about the life or death of Joseph. Medieval legend, however, says that Joseph was sent to England to establish Christianity and that he took the Holy Grail to that country.

JOSEPH OF ARIMATHAEA, James J. Tissot (1836–1902). © SuperStock (999-9319).

JOSEPH OF ARIMATHAEA

PAM KENNEDY

My life was one of conflict. Torn between my hesitancy and a desire to act upon my convictions, I walked a tightrope between cowardice and courage, struggling to be free from guilt. And then one day, convinced I had missed my last opportunity for inner peace, I learned a lesson only God could teach.

Like my heart, Jerusalem was a place of contradiction. In the polished courts of the temple, priests in jeweled robes accepted offerings from those seeking forgiveness while the oily smoke from their sacrificial fires seeped into dingy alleys. Beggars reached out gnarled hands for mercy as busy lawyers, on their way to argue for justice, swept past without a glance. And I, Joseph of Arimathaea, a member of the Jewish Supreme Court, spent my life debating legal minutiae.

It was within this court, the Sanhedrin, that the seeds of both my cowardice and courage took root. A debate had raged for months over the recent popularity of a man some claimed to be the Messiah. Most of my colleagues found these claims blasphemous and the man himself worthy of death. Additionally, they felt a personal threat as he taught a doctrine at odds with the ancient ways, threatening destruction on us religious leaders for our corruption of God's Law.

The problem was with the people. He was immensely popular, and hundreds followed him everywhere as each week brought new accounts of his miracles, healings, and exorcisms. In our chamber the heated debate continued as one after another rose to express contempt for this itinerant, uneducated rabbi from Nazareth. Unwilling to cast an uninformed ballot, I determined to investigate the troublemaker for myself.

Day after day I stood with the rabble surrounding Jesus, listening to his teaching, watching his face, examining his interaction with the people clamoring for his attention. And day by day I became more convinced that this uneducated rabbi was unique. He spoke with authority about forgiveness and reconciliation, healing and compassion. He urged his followers to obey the spirit, not just the words, of the ancient Law and to be willing to lay down their lives for their friends. He was patient and kind, but never weak. And as I listened, something burned within my heart. It dawned on me that he did more than just speak the truth; I realized he was the truth.

But what could I do? My peers had made their positions clear. I risked expulsion from the Sanhedrin by siding with this rebel. The ancient traditions of my culture bound me tighter than my newfound hope. Tentative, I spoke privately to a colleague who had once stood before the council suggesting we ignore this so-called prophet, until time proved him either true or false. Placing his arm about my shoulders, Nicodemus related a midnight conversation with Jesus. He said the man had spoken to him of a new birth only experienced by those with true faith. His heart was as moved as mine he said; but like myself, he remained silent. What could it hurt to wait just a little longer?

Then, one night during Passover week, the president of the Sanhedrin called an emergency meeting. In a frenzy born of desperate fear and anger, arguments echoed through the chamber. "He must be stopped!" "The people are ready to declare him King!" "The Romans will kill us all!" "Better one to die than everyone!"

Suddenly I stood, found my voice, and loudly cast my vote against the majority. Shocked silence, then murmurs, then shouting swallowed up my plea. It was too late. In a few moments it was over. The condemnation held, and those thirsty for blood ran from the chamber to plead their case before the Roman procurator, Pilate.

Scarcely twelve hours later, I stood on a small hillside called Golgotha and watched the Son of God die on a wooden cross. Once more I was silent, strangled this time by guilt.

I watched the sky turn dark, women weep, soldiers gamble for his only piece of clothing. And I heard the words that still whisper in my soul: "Father forgive them." I knew they were meant for me. The earth heaved with anguish and a voice cried, "It is finished."

Screaming as if in pain, I ran to Pilate's courtyard, beat upon the locked gates, and insisted on an audience before the proconsul.

"Give me the body of the Christ!" I demanded.

Unwilling to meet Jesus while he lived, I could now only reach out to him in death. Pilate's signed permission in hand, I ran to fetch Nicodemus, and together we raced back to the hill outside the city to claim the body of the Lord.

We lifted the lifeless form from the cross and tenderly wrapped it in strips of fine, clean linen. Then, bearing the body I knew I had helped to slay, I placed it in the tomb prepared for my own burial. Silently we backed out of the limestone cave, sealing the opening with a huge boulder.

I returned to my home, heavy with self-condemnation and regret, and fell upon my bed. It was there Nicodemus found me the morning after the Sabbath. Excited, he told me of the miracle reported by the women. Together we raced to see for ourselves and found it was just as they had said: The boulder was moved! The tomb was empty!

In the weeks that followed, we saw the

risen Christ, walked with him, and finally understood the ancient promises of God with hearts reborn. It was then I realized that overshadowing all my failure is his victory and the blessed assurance that I am beloved by God, forever forgiven. It was then I learned the lesson of the Resurrection: With God, it is never too late.

When the even was come, there came a rich man of Arimathaea, named Joseph, who also himself was Jesus' disciple: He went to Pilate, and begged the body of Jesus. Then Pilate commanded the body to be delivered. And when Joseph had taken the body, he wrapped it in a clean linen cloth, And laid it in his own new tomb, which he had hewn out in the rock: and he rolled a great stone to the door of the sepulchre, and departed. And there was Mary Magdalene, and the other Mary, sitting over against the sepulchre (MATTHEW 27:57–61).

JOSEPH OF ARIMATHAEA IN PILATE'S HOUSE, James J. Tissot (1836–1902). © SuperStock (999-318).

THE SILVER CHALICE

THOMAS B. COSTAIN

The summons came at one o'clock, but the talking had not reached an end when Basil arrived at the spacious room of the head of the house. He recognized the deep voice of Paul as soon as the door opened to admit him.

"I will not compromise, Joseph of Arimathaea," the Apostle was saying. "I have come to Jerusalem with a message. A message for your stiff-necked leaders, for such they are in very truth. It is this—that the Gentiles must be received, not on our terms but on their own terms. They must not be compelled to accept everything in the Law of Moses. To us the Law is familiar. It seems to us perfect. We were born to it and we believe in it. But to the Gentiles it is strange and frightening and it would drive them away from Christ. If we say they must be circumcised before they may belong, they will turn their backs on the great truths which Jesus taught. No, no, Joseph of Arimathaea, I must be firm and allow no tampering with the decision reached five years ago, at which time I was given a free hand. The second thoughts, the reservations, which now fill the minds of the presbyters of the faith, must be put aside."

"This is the young man," said Joseph, motioning Basil to enter.

As Basil made his way into the room, he saw that Joseph was reclining on his couch as usual and that both Luke and Deborra were present, although seated at a distance. Paul, who was stationed close to Joseph, turned at his entrance and gave him the benefit of a quick but intent glance.

The first close glimpse that Basil was thus afforded of this remarkable man was in the nature of a shock. He was surprised to find how old the great Apostle had become. Paul's hair and beard were white, and there were both fatigue and suffering in the lines clustering about his eyes and accenting the hollowness of his cheeks. It surprised the youth also that the face that had been turned to him was not an agreeable one. The features seemed to have been cut out of the hardest granite, and the expression was stern. But at the same time he realized it was a compelling face. The eyes under straight white brows were the color of the moon in a

And he took the cup, and gave thanks, and gave it to them, saying, Drink ye all of it; For this is my blood of the new testament, which is shed for many for the remission of sins. (MATTHEW 26:27–28).

daylight sky, strange eyes, disturbing and at the same time fascinating.

Basil realized after one glance at this frail old man, in his short and unadorned woolen tunic, that no one else in the room seemed to matter.

Joseph cleared his throat. "I have already said that I am pleased with what this young man has done for me. There is something I have not told you." He motioned toward the clay bust, which stood on a pedestal beside him. "It was not for this alone that I had him come here. There is something of much more moment to be done. It is so vital that I had to be sure of the artist who would undertake it. "This," indicating the clay head, "was a test. He has passed it so well that I am sure he is capable of the much greater work that is now to be done.

"I have been making another test," went on the venerable head of the house. "It was not enough to be sure of this young man's skill with his hands. I had to be equally sure of him—of his character, his loyalty, his patience, even his courage. Unknown to him, I think, he has been under observation. I wish to say now that he has satisfied me on every point."

Basil saw that Luke was smiling and nodding his head at him. Deborra was leaning forward, her lips slightly parted in anxious anticipation.

"Young man," said Joseph, addressing Basil directly, "I must tell you, before going any further, that the task I have in mind would entail the most careful study and the hardest of work. You must give years to it if necessary. You must travel, for there are many men to be seen, of whom you must make as good likenesses as you have of me. You must expect to meet opposition and to face danger."

"I shall be happy to undertake it," declared Basil. "And to give every moment of my time to it. If I have any reluctance at all, it is because I wonder if it will be possible to satisfy you." He paused and then asked, "Where would it be necessary for me to go?"

"To Caesarea, I think. To Ephesus. Perhaps to Rome."

Basil found it hard to prevent himself from crying out exultantly, "I will go! That he would have to visit Rome was sufficient to make him accept instantly. The answer to the question that had been weighing heaviest on his mind had been found. He would get to Rome. . . .

The main explanation was now to be made. Joseph glanced first at Paul and then at Luke. "Some years ago an object came into my possession," he said. "It was of such a nature that I trembled at the responsibility that had been placed on me. The fear that it might suffer damage or that it might—ah, what a terrifying thought!— be stolen or lost weighed so on my mind that I had a special room made in which to keep it. There it has been ever since, as free of observation as though in the Holy of Holies. Today, for the first time, I propose to open the room."

Paul had listened to the explanation with interest but also with some impatience. It was clear he resented the interruption to the discussion of his views. "My good Joseph, what can this most mysterious object be?" he asked.

"Let me tell you first," said Joseph, "how it came into my hands. A woman brought it to me, a humble woman who had hidden it away, not being sure of her duty in the matter. She had feared it might get into the wrong hands and so she had waited. It was with the most solemn admonitions that she confided it to me. I was to keep it until I in turn could be sure of what was to be done. She was very poor, but I need hardly tell you that she refused any remuneration."

Joseph made an effort to rise from his couch but found that he needed assistance in getting to his feet. With Deborra supporting him on one side and Basil on the other, he began to cross the room.

"I am old," he said, sighing. "Old and stiff. May I say to you, Paul of Tarsus, and to you, my good friend Luke, that to have had this sacred object in my possession has been such an honor that I am conscious of my unworthiness."

He walked slowly to the far wall of the room and stretched out his hand in search of a spring concealed behind an old chest of acacia wood. The pressure of his fingers caused a panel in the wall to roll back. Behind it was a small, unlighted space, a few feet square only.

"A lamp, if you please, my child," said the old man.

Deborra brought one and held it inside the dark cubicle. It could be seen then that the space was occupied by a box of sandalwood standing on a pedestal of marble. Joseph reached an arm within and raised the gold-studded lid of the box. From it he produced a drinking cup, a small and very plain cup.

It was ovoid in shape and made of silver. The design was of the simplest, for the lip had been turned over with the hastiest workmanship and no attempt whatever at ornamentation. It had seen much service, obviously, for it was battered and marked, particularly on the lip.

He held it out for their inspection in hands that trembled with reverence and excitement.

"This," he said in a whisper, "is the cup from which Jesus drank and then passed to his devoted followers at the Last Supper."

THE LAST SUPPER, Peter Paul Rubens (1577–1640), Pinacoteca di Brera, Milan, Italy.
© Pinacoteca di Brera/ SuperStock (263-3).

BENEATH THE CROSS

THE APOSTLES

When Jesus had thus said, he was troubled in spirit, and testified, and said, Verily, verily, I say unto you, that one of you shall betray me. Then the disciples looked one on another, doubting of whom he spake. Now there was leaning on Jesus' bosom one of his disciples, whom Jesus loved. Simon Peter therefore beckoned to him, that he should ask who it should be of whom he spake. He then lying on Jesus' breast saith unto him, Lord, who is it? Jesus answered, He it is, to whom I shall give a sop, when I have dipped it. And when he had dipped the sop, he gave it to Judas Iscariot, the son of Simon. And after the sop Satan entered into him. Then said Jesus unto him, That thou doest, do quickly (JOHN 13:21–27).

THE DISPERSION OF THE APOSTLES, Charles Gleyre (1806–1874), Musee Girodet, Montargis. © Musee Girodet,Montargis/SuperStock (1158-1248).

Judas Iscariot
I, Judas

Taylor Caldwell and Jesse Stearn

The confrontation had come at last. In a few hours, before the Passover, the world would know of Christ's power. He was not always a peaceful man. I had seen his eye flash at injustice and, risking Roman wrath, he had pulled their victims from the trees to which they had been nailed for not paying Rome its tribute or for striking a Roman soldier who trifled with their women. He would yet be a Moses to his people, that I felt, despite all his talk of dying. He who raised Lazarus could surely raise himself. Even if he did everything only with the Father's help, certainly the God that helped Moses, assailing the Egyptians with pestilence and flood, would not forsake his only begotten son.

I could see no reason for the elaborate preparations to take him. Scores of Temple guards had been mustered and Pilate's troops had been put on an alert. There was also a multitude of Levites and Temple sympathizers who were to trail along to counter any opposing opinion. But who would be there at this hour, in the lonely Garden of Gethsemane, among the abandoned olive presses, but Jesus and the Twelve? What Twelve? I winced in spite of myself.

The time had come for Jesus to take a stand. . . . The guards carried lanterns and torches, and some were armed with swords and staves. I knew exactly where to take them, having been in the Garden of Gethsemane many times, and soon, walking rapidly with Malchus at my elbow, I made out the shadow of a lone figure near an ebbing fire. Even from the silhouette, I knew who it must be.

As we burst into the camp, the place immediately came alive. One person after another scrambled up from his bed of grass and rent the night with cries of alarm. The captain of the Temple guards was straining in the darkness.

"I will pick him out for you," I whispered. "Whomsoever I kiss, it shall be he. Hold him fast so that he will suffer no injury from your soldiers."

Jesus stood quietly, as though he had been waiting for me.

I leaned forward and kissed him on the cheek. He gave me a look that made my knees tremble.

"My dear friend," said he, "I have been expecting you. You see, I threw the sop rightly."

I was beside myself with grief. "Master, Master," I cried.

THE TAKING OF CHRIST, Jean Valentin de Boulogne, Museum of Fine Arts, Boston, Massachusetts.
© Museum of Fine Arts, Boston, Massachusetts/SuperStock (900°875).

And this they took for a sign. But he bore no malice, this I know, for he held out his hand to me first; no disciple took Jesus' hand of himself. "Do what you have to, and do it fast," he said, for he knew that what I did was not out of spite but for what he might do.

"This is no betrayal, Master," I whispered in his ear. "Trust me. For if you but raise your voice for freedom, all will still follow you, even the Temple guards."

He turned away from me, and from the clustered lights of many torches I could see his eyes flash boldly over the multitude.

"Why do you come as though I were a thief? Have I not sat daily with you teaching in the Temple, and you made no effort to lay hold of me?

The multitude fell back, and even the soldiers sank to their knees in their fear. . . .

They did not take the time to deliberate. "Death, death, death." It was almost a chorus. And each time the word rang out, I felt a lump in my throat. Not "guilty," but "death," they voted, though they could not execute the sentence themselves. Had this responsibility been theirs, perhaps they would have hesitated in their judgment.

The verdict did not appear to affect Jesus. As he was being blindfolded as a condemned man, to be led away to Pilate, he made no protest. My eyes searched his imploringly, but he seemed not to notice. He was letting them do what they wanted with him. . . .

"Come forward," [Caiaphas] ordered peremptorily. As I moved up to the platform, he reached under his desk and brought out a pouch.

"Come, take this," he cried. "It is yours."

I stretched out my hand uncertainly. It was heavy and it jangled.

"You must know what it is. You hold the purse strings for this company of beggars."

I suddenly realized what was in the bag.

I shrank back. "I want none of it."

"Take it," he commanded. "It is the price for your service, the traditional payment for information leading to the conviction of an enemy of the people."

He pulled me by the arm. "Count it well; there are thirty pieces of silver therein."

"Make haste," bellowed Caiaphas, "the Passover will be here while you gloat over your reward."

"I do not want it," I cried. "Take it from me."

"You have no choice," said Annas, "it is the law. Put it in the bag with the money you have gathered for the Son of God."

I could have wept in my shame, for I had committed no betrayal, despite how it looked. Jesus could still save himself before Pilate, that I knew, if only he would consider the many who rested their hopes on him. I turned to him, but his eyes were covered and he saw no more. . . .

From my first memory I dreamed of a Messiah. I stood in the holy Temple and implored God that these eyes of mine might behold his promised. My heart was uplifted before I became a man at the age of thirteen, for in my soul I heard his assurance that I would see his Son.

I encountered Joshua-bar-Joseph in a little town on the Jordan when I was searching for the Messiah. I had dreamt that I saw him, all glorious and beautiful, radiant with holiness and the Godhead, and when I saw him in truth I believed it was he.

I left my house and my mother and my estates for him. I followed him and exulted in him, and his words were as sweet as the juice of a pomegranate, and as living as honey and as fulfilling as milk and manna, and as tender as the flesh of the date. I saw his miracles, and heard the resonance of his great voice, and all who saw him were amazed, even those who hated him. Yet he carried no golden rod of authority and power, no carved ivory staff, and there was no crown on his head. But my heart leapt at the sight of him, my soul rejoiced, and I said in my heart: "He has come!" A poor carpenter, they said of him, a man of no consequence, a barefoot rabbi, a peasant, a humble creature. . . .

None loved him as I loved him. None who followed him was as I, a Pharisee of a noble family, a man of wealth and gold, honored in the holy places. The others were miserable people of no learning and family. I suffered agonies of impatience when they could not understand his words, which, though apparently simple, were profound and strange and oblique. But I understood. There were times when the others bent their foolish heads and silently mouthed his words, and shook their ragged locks, but he looked at me and faintly smiled and knew that I understood what he had said. Then my soul would burn with joy at the meeting of our eyes, and I was exalted and we exchanged smile for smile, though his smile was shadowed with sadness. . . . .

How dared the rabble touch him, speak with him, walk in his footsteps, importune him, follow him, hold up their miserable children for his blessing, put their hands on his garments? How dared they ask him to cure their sick? Among them were the very Roman centurions and their officers, and even the judges and the scribes, and often, to my amazement, my fellow Pharisees. How dared

the humble offer him wine and fruit and dates and bread and fish and meat? It was an offense that cried to God for punishment for the sacrilege. Why did he condescend to walk into the houses of the tax gathers, the oppressors hired by the Romans to afflict starving Israel, those who took the very bread from the mouths of the Jews? They were criminals, these tax gatherers, who, for a few shekels, drove their fellow Jews to penury and despair. Yet he suffered them and had compassion for these jackals, these most accursed of God—these whores of the Romans!

Would God have pity on those who afflicted his people? Once I spoke of this, and he said: "The righteous have their own reward in their souls, but the evil must be lifted from darkness and delivered to the light." Then he gazed at me, and there was great sorrow in his beautiful eyes. . . .

But, as I stand here below the tree under which I will die, I cannot help but wonder. Is he indeed the Messiah? Is he indeed the hope of man, the promise of God? Have I deceived myself, or is he the truth?

In death only is the answer. My question may be answered. It may not. In any event, I will be at peace. . . .

I come quickly, dear God, as even so came Jesus. Accept me, Lord, for I sinned in my pride, and in that pride, I knew not what I did. May Jesus Christ be with all, as he was with me. Amen.

JUDAS BETRAYING JESUS WITH A KISS, James J. Tissot(1806–1902). © SuperStock (999-234).

JUDAS ISCARIOT

H. A. GUY

> Then Judas, which had betrayed him, when he saw that he was condemned, repented himself, and brought again the thirty pieces of silver to the chief priests and elders, Saying, I have sinned in that I have betrayed the innocent blood. And they said, What is that to us? see thou to that. And he cast down the pieces of silver in the temple, and departed, and went and hanged himself. And the chief priests took the silver pieces, and said, It is not lawful for to put them into the treasury, because it is the price of blood. And they took counsel, and bought with them the potter's field, to bury strangers in (MATTHEW 27:3–7).

In all the lists of the Apostles his name comes last, with the addition of "the traitor." . . . There are two accounts of the death of Judas. In the Acts of the Apostles, the author reports (in the course of a speech by Peter suggesting a successor to Judas) that he bought a field with the money he received and fell in it, apparently by accident, and died. The field was hence called Akeldama—"the field of blood." But Matthew says that Judas returned the money to the priests and with it they bought a field to bury foreigners in, while Judas hanged himself. . . .

Various attempts have been made to account for Judas' behavior. John suggests that it was greed and also that he was inspired by the devil (John 13:2). Some have thought that Judas wanted to force Jesus' hand and to prompt him to deliver himself from his enemies. Many have considered that Judas was disappointed by Jesus' refusal to establish a kingdom by force. There is no real evidence for this view. Probably Judas' motives were mixed. If he was a southerner, he may have felt "out of it" among the Galileans or considered himself superior to them. He may have been jealous of Jesus' favor for other disciples such as Peter. It may have been simply spite which prompted him to go to the priests. There must have been great possibilities for good in him, for Jesus to have chosen him as one of his intimate company.

PETER
SIMON PETER, THE ROCK

PAM KENNEDY

Peter leaned toward the fire, extending his hands against the heat. His palms burned, but the chill of foreboding and dread, the icy pain of self-doubt and blame, still filled his chest. So much had happened in just a few hours. He recalled the warmth of fellowship in the upper room and how it had been shattered by Jesus' announcement that he would soon be betrayed. When Peter protested, declaring his devotion, the Master only shook his head sadly and predicted that even Peter would disown him three times before the cock crowed. The shame of those words still stung.

Later, in Gethsemane, Peter was unable even to stay awake while Jesus prayed. His heart ached under the gentle rebuke of the one he loved and served. And then when Judas led the angry mob to arrest Jesus, Peter tried to defend his Master, lopping off the ear of Malchus, servant to the high priest. Jesus' touch healed the servant's ear, but his words wounded the impulsive disciple once again: "Put your sword away! Shall I not drink the cup the Father has given me?"

Now, in the courtyard of the high priest, Peter shivered near the fire. Somewhere inside the walls Jesus was being questioned, perhaps even beaten, and here in fear and shame sat the disciple who had vowed to follow him even to death. Jesus once called him Peter, the rock. He had once walked on water, even cast out demons and healed the sick through the power of God. Now he longed only to hide within the shadows.

"Aren't you one of his disciples?"

Peter, startled from his thoughts, looked up at the servant girl quickly. "No!" he replied, "You must be mistaken."

She studied him a moment, then moved on. Peter felt sweat break out on his forehead. He noted the glances of the others near the fire and shifted his position in an effort to appear unconcerned.

"Didn't I see you in the garden at the time of the man's arrest?"

Peter's heart pounded in his ears, and he raised his voice to drown it out. "No! I tell you I don't know the man!" He rose in anger and stalked across the courtyard to the gate.

The others, like hunters cornering their prey, followed him. One approached with a malevolent and triumphant expression and announced to the others, "You can tell by his Galilean accent that he's one of them."

In a desperate fury, Peter shook his fist and swore, "I don't even know who you are

DENIAL OF SAINT PETER, Rembrandt Harmensz van Rijn (1606–1669), Rijksmuseum Vincent van Gogh, Amsterdam.
© Rijksmuseum Vincent van Gogh, Amsterdam/SuperStock (900–526).

talking about!"

His fist was still in the air when a rooster's crow echoed in the courtyard. The sound pierced Peter's heart as the words of Christ raced through his mind: "Before the cock crows, you will disown me three times." Blindly, he fumbled with the iron gate, stumbling into the darkness beyond.

Like a man possessed, Peter ran through the dark streets of Jerusalem, his breath coming in sobs. Reaching the house where the disciples had taken the Passover, he dashed up the stone stairway to the upper room, pushed open the heavy wooden door, entered and bolted it behind him. In the dimness he saw the alarm on the faces of several of the other disciples. Peter collapsed in the corner of the room hiding his face in his hands.

For two days and nights the frightened disciples cowered in the upper room. They clung to each other when the earth shook at midday and listened in awe as John returned from the crucifixion to relate the scene and recount their Lord's last words. No one dared to leave; their meals were eaten in solemn silence, each one lost in his own thoughts and fears.

On the morning of the first day of the week, shortly after dawn, there was a pounding at the door. Carefully, Peter opened it a crack. Mary of Magdala pushed past him, her face alight with wonder, her breath coming in rapid bursts.

"I have seen the Lord!" she announced. "He is alive. He has risen from the dead!" She wheeled around and pointed at the dumbfounded fishermen. "And there was an angel who said you should all go to Galilee because Jesus would meet you there!" Mary's eyes blazed with an unearthly fervor, and tendrils of dark hair clung to her flushed cheeks.

One of the men leaned toward her and whispered, "You are mad, woman. Your grief has overcome you. The Master is dead. John saw it all at Golgotha."

"No, no! You don't understand! He was dead, but now he's not!" She looked imploringly at the incredulous men. "The tomb is empty, I tell you. Our Lord lives!"

Mary dashed past Peter and disappeared down the stairway in a rush of flapping robes as she hastily threw her veil over her hair.

Peter stared at the open door, Mary's words echoing in his mind: The tomb empty? The Lord alive?

Suddenly, John ran through the doorway and Peter's indecision dissipated. He followed after the other disciple, trailing him through the streets until they reached the tomb. John stopped at the opening, staring into the darkness within; but Peter, impelled by his unreasonable hope, dashed into the sepulcher and then froze, gaping at the scene before him. On the stony bier lay the linen bindings that Joseph and Nicodemus had lovingly wrapped around Jesus' body only a few days earlier. The wrappings were undisturbed, still wound as if around a form, but empty and limp. It was as if the body had evaporated, leaving the burial cloths like an empty shell.

Peter was aware of movement behind him and turned to see John approaching the bier. John's face registered incredulity at first and then a light of understanding began to dawn. The men looked at one another, then John gripped Peter's arm.

"It's true!" he whispered.

Peter nodded slowly, his mind racing to grasp what his heart was already beginning to accept. If the Lord is alive, there is hope—hope for forgiveness, for restoration, for healing. If the Lord is alive, Peter could be freed from his prison of regret and guilt; freed to be the rock that Jesus had once challenged him to become. Peter had entered that room of death a broken, empty man, but he would leave it whole and filled. If Jesus is alive, nothing is impossible.

Then took they him, and led him, and brought him into the high priest's house. And Peter followed afar off. And when they had kindled a fire in the midst of the hall, and were set down together, Peter sat down among them. But a certain maid beheld him as he sat by the fire, and earnestly looked upon him, and said, This man was also with him. And he denied him, saying, Woman, I know him not. And after a little while another saw him, and said, Thou art also of them. And Peter said, Man, I am not. And about the space of one hour after another confidently affirmed, saying, Of a truth this fellow also was with him: for he is a Galilean. And Peter said, Man, I know not what thou sayest. And immediately, while he yet spake, the cock crew. And the Lord turned, and looked upon Peter. And Peter remembered the word of the Lord, how he had said unto him, Before the cock crow, thou shalt deny me thrice. And Peter went out, and wept bitterly (LUKE 22:54–62).

THE BIG FISHERMAN

LLOYD C. DOUGLAS

And now it was Wednesday morning. Thad had gone ashore on an errand. Simon's knees were lame from his unaccustomed exercise, and after an hour of it he came wearily to his feet and walked the length of the deck, wondering what had detained the boy. Three dories were on the water, and moving rapidly, their oars flashing in the sun. With narrowed eyes, shaded by his cupped hands, Simon identified the occupants of the boats. Thad was bringing Andrew. James and John were in the second dory which had overtaken and was now passing Thad. Lagging behind came Philip with Thomas and old Bartholomew.

Simon's heart was in his throat. How could he face these men? They were drawing closer now, near enough for him to see their animation. They seemed happy! Whatever could have happened? He tossed a rope to the first dory and Johnny scrambled up, flung a leg over the rail and threw his arms around the bewildered skipper.

"You haven't heard!" he shouted, exultantly. "You don't know! Listen!

Jesus lives! . . . I tell you—he is alive!"

James had grasped Simon's arm.

"We have seen him, Peter! He came to us—Sunday night—at Benyosef's house!"

They had all swarmed over the rail now, all but Bartholomew who was being tugged on board by Thad. Simon stood there dazed, his lips quivering, the tears running down his cheeks.

"He told us to make haste, and go home," said Philip. "He was anxious for you to know."

"That's what he said," put in Johnny. "He said, 'Go and tell Peter!'"

"Are you sure he said 'Peter'?" asked the Big Fisherman, huskily.

"Aye! That he did!" declared Bartholomew. "'Go—quickly—and tell Peter!'"

"Where is he now?" entreated Peter. "I must go to him!"

"We're to wait here," said Andrew. "He is coming to us."

At the first gray-blue light before dawn, the Big Fisherman rose and walked forward. It was still too early to identify the familiar landmarks. On such a morning, he had stood here gazing

Then Jesus saith unto them, Children, have ye any meat? They answered him, No. And he said unto them, Cast the net on the right side of the ship, and ye shall find. They cast therefore, and now they were not able to draw it for the multitude of fishes (JOHN 21:5–6).

MIRACULOUS DRAUGHT OF FISHES, Raphael (1483–1520). National Gallery, London, England.
© National Gallery, London/SuperStock (900-723).

toward the shore in the pre-dawn haze and had heard a voice calling "Simon!" With what heart-racing haste had he scrambled into the little boat and flailed the lake with excited oars! And then he had received his commission as the fisherman who would now "fish for men."

The sky was brightening a little and the fog was dissolving. Dimly the outlines of the wharves and huts became visible. The Big Fisherman's narrowed eyes slowly swept the shoreline. A tall, slender column of blue smoke was rising from a small, bright fire at the water's edge. Beside the fire, warming his hands, stood the Master. He raised his arm, waved a hand, and called:

"Peter!"

THE POWER TO CHANGE

PAM KENNEDY

Mara stands just outside the circle of light cast by the fire, watching the men gathered to warm themselves and talk. There is urgency in their conversation. A little while earlier several of the guards of her master, Caiaphas, had burst into the courtyard, leading a prisoner known as Jesus the Nazarene. They were followed by a group of Temple leaders who loudly demanded to be taken to the high priest immediately. The religious men disappeared with the prisoner into the inner chambers; but now the guards gather in the courtyard along with some of the other servants, and they sit gossiping by the fire. Another fellow, a stranger, sits among them, silent, watchful, nervous, and Mara focuses her attention upon him. He is large and rugged looking, with rough hands and brown, muscular arms. When he speaks, refusing a drink from the goatskin full of wine, Mara recognizes his accent as Galilean. Suddenly she makes the connection.

"You were with the prisoner. You are one of his followers!" Her voice startles the men, and they stare first at her and then at the stranger sitting among them.

The man looks like an animal trapped in a corner. His dark eyes dart from face to face, and he shakes his head vehemently. "I don't know what you're talking about."

"Yes, you do," Mara insists, stepping toward him. "You even sound like the prisoner. Your accent gives you away."

Now they are the center of attention, the slave girl and this rough-looking man from Galilee. She will not be humiliated in front of her fellow servants and the guards. She lifts an accusatory finger and points at him as he stands. "You're as guilty as he is. Why won't you admit it?"

The man stumbles backward from the group; and at that moment, the door from the high priest's chambers bursts open, and two armed men shove the beaten and stumbling Jesus into the courtyard. There is a moment when time seems to stop. The prisoner and the stranger stand staring at one another, and Mara thinks she sees a flash of recogni-

> And Peter said, Man, I know not what thou sayest. And immediately, while he yet spake, the cock crew. And the Lord turned, and looked upon Peter. And Peter remembered the word of the Lord, how he had said unto him, Before the cock crow, thou shalt deny me thrice. And Peter went out, and wept bitterly (LUKE 22:60–62).

tion. Then a rooster somewhere crows twice, rending the pre-dawn stillness. The prisoner turns away; the stranger gasps, then flees from the courtyard as if pursued by demons. Mara hears his anguished cries echoing off the courtyard walls long after he is gone.

It has been almost seven weeks since the arrest and crucifixion of Jesus, the man some called the Christ. Many in Jerusalem have forgotten about him. There is always some new local celebrity claiming to be the Messiah. Most come and go, and no one pays them much attention. Mara keeps to herself, busy with her responsibilities in the house of the high priest. But today is the first day of Pentecost, and she rushes to the marketplace to do her shopping for the household before the sun becomes unbearably hot. The streets teem with visitors from distant countries. Their unfamiliar languages swirl around Mara like dissonant melodies. She loves the marketplace with its myriad scents and sounds, for here she can briefly pretend she is the mistress of her own home, purchasing vegetables and meat to prepare for a husband and children. For a little while she dreams of such contentment, but reality always intrudes. If she doesn't hurry, the high priest's wife will be angry. She turns her attention to a basket of fresh onions.

"Hurry, I tell you, it's a miracle!" A man pushes past Mara, almost knocking her over. She turns to see people from the market dashing along the street, all shouting and talking in a variety of languages.

She grasps the robe of a woman rushing by. "What is it? Where are you going?" The woman stops for a moment and says something about fire and rushing wind and men from Jerusalem speaking in languages they had never learned, giving the people a message from God himself.

Mara joins the throng and is swept along to an area in front of a two-story house. A man stands, raises his arms, and speaks in a loud voice. "People of Israel, listen! God publicly endorsed Jesus of Nazareth by doing miracles, wonders, and signs, but you, with the help of the Gentiles, nailed him to a cross and killed him. Now I stand here declaring that God released him from the horrors of death and raised him back to life again."

Mara stares, and her mouth falls open in astonishment. The man speaking is that same one who denied he even knew Jesus and then fled sobbing from the courtyard just a few weeks earlier. Today he stands in the midst of thousands, boldly declaring his belief that Jesus is God's true son! The young woman wonders at the transformation as she stands listening to Peter the fisherman. His words penetrate her heart as nothing ever has. He speaks of hope and forgiveness, of living guided by God's own spirit. It is as if he pours water on the dried and shriveled dreams deep in Mara's heart. She who has only, always, been a worthless slave, hears that she is precious and worthy of God's love. And she believes it.

She loses track of time and begins to hear a new voice, first from outside, then from within, telling her she can begin life anew. She can be free. She, Mara, is a person of value, not just a possession to be used and cast aside when her master tires of her. When Peter stops speaking, the cries of Mara and the others rise in the dusty afternoon: "What should we do? What should we do?"

"Come," he says. And they follow Peter and are baptized, joining together in a community of believers. Mara still serves, but now from a heart filled with love, as the daughter of a king. Together with thousands who heard Peter's words at Pentecost, she becomes part of a brand-new family. It is a family that learns and eats and shares all they have together. It is a family that will change the world because of their Father's love.

PETER'S DENIAL, Robert Leinweber (1845–1915). © SuperStock (900–4603).

Saint Peter, Gerard Seghers (1591–1651). Louvre, Paris, France.
© Reunion des Musees Nationaux/Art Resource (ART147280).

> And Jesus, walking by the sea of Galilee, saw two brethren, Simon called Peter, and Andrew his brother, casting a net into the sea: for they were fishers. And he saith unto them, Follow me, and I will make you fishers of men. And they straightway left their nets, and followed him (MATTHEW 4:18–20).

PETER

LANDRUM P. LEAVELL

Simon Peter was a typical young commercial fisherman. He was deft in the use of his hands, those same hands which were sometimes used in violence. His temperament had taken on the characteristics of the Lake of Gennesaret or the Sea of Galilee or the Sea of Tiberias as it is variously called in the New Testament. He was subject to ever-changing moods, and on occasion his temperament was fiery. He had a sharp tongue and all who knew him knew he had an opinion on every subject. He was not always right, but he was always vocal. . . .

When Peter makes his first New Testament appearance, he is called Simon. This is the Gentile or Greek version of the name Simeon. On at least two occasions in the New Testament he is referred to as Simeon, which is the original Hebrew form of the name. On occasion in the New Testament, Peter is referred to as Cephas, for Jesus gave Simon a new name. The name Jesus gave him is ordinarily rendered Peter, from the Greek word *petros* which means "rock." Cephas is the Aramaic version of that same word. . . .

In many of the New Testament accounts of Peter, we see him in contrast. He was both brave and cowardly, wise and foolish, fearful and fearless, open-minded and closed-minded, a man of doubt and a man of faith. He was impulsive and uninhibited, often speaking before he thought. . . .

Peter had a spiritual perception which is enviable. He, out of the twelve, was the only one who understood fully the identity of Jesus Christ. He knew who Jesus was and was not afraid to state it. What a matchless moment that must have been to hear Jesus Christ say, "Blessed art thou, Simon Bar-jona: for flesh and blood hath not revealed it unto thee."

PETER AND JOHN

Robert Hoyer

John and I were together on Easter Sunday morning, silent and brooding. What was there to talk about? What John thought I do not know. I sat in bitterness and counted up the shards of a life that was lost. I planned to move to another country, where I was not known, and pretend before men that I was still strong. And Mary came breathless to the door. She had been to the grave to complete the burial, and the soldiers were gone and the stone was rolled away. Someone must have removed the body of Jesus. We waited to hear no more—we jumped to our feet and ran. And to further cut my wounded pride, there came the distress of age; I had to say: "You go on, John; I cannot run so fast." And he outran me to the grave. But when I arrived, John was still outside. I was amazed. "Does he still wait for me to lead?" I thought, and bluntly ran right into the grave itself. On the shelf where Jesus had been placed, the grave clothes lay, empty, flat, and undisturbed; just as they had been wrapped about the body of my Lord.

The evidence was plain—Jesus had risen from the dead. It was certainly no grave robbery, no simple reburial. It would have been silly and impossible to remove the body without the winding-sheet. And it was no dream or vision; my pounding heart and laboring breath, the feel of the cold stone beneath my hand, were far too real for that. Jesus had risen from the dead, and my leadership was needed once again; for this men must know and believe: Jesus had risen from dead.

A frantic hope was born within my heart, but that hope gave birth to fear. For I had been revealed a weakling and a failure to him who had called me "Rock." Would he want me as his disciple again? Would he count on me for anything? I remembered what he told me: "I have prayed for you, that your faith fail not," and my faith had failed. I remembered his look in the courtyard of Caiaphas. And the women came with the message of the angel: "Tell his disciples—and Peter—that he will meet them in Galilee."

Those were my darkest moments. I had been ashamed of my own weakness, but I had not been afraid. Now I had reason for weeping—now I was afraid. Now—O God—because there was hope in Christ, my denial was doubly evil. Because there was hope in Christ, my agony increased tenfold. I had not denied a failure; I had denied the Christ the Son of God, the Lord of life and death.

So hope gave birth to fear, and I knelt to pray. I remembered the story Jesus told, and I laid my heart and all its selfish secrets open to

CHRIST'S CHARGE TO PETER, Peter Paul Rubens (1577-1640), WALLACE COLLECTION, LONDON, ENGLAND. © WALLACE COLLECTION, LONDON/SUPERSTOCK (900-132623).

Peter therefore went forth, and that other disciple, and came to the sepulchre. So they ran both together: and the other disciple did outrun Peter, and came first to the sepulchre. And he stooping down, and looking in, saw the linen clothes lying; yet went he not in. Then cometh Simon Peter following him, and went into the sepulchre, and seeth the linen clothes lie, And the napkin, that was about his head, not lying with the linen clothes, but wrapped together in a place by itself. Then went in also that other disciple, which came first to the sepulchre, and he saw, and believed. For as yet they knew not the scripture, that he must rise again from the dead. Then the disciples went away again unto their own home (JOHN 20:3–10).

my Lord: "God, be merciful to me, a sinner." My leadership was vanity; it was pride and selfishness that closed my heart to love. All that I had been was false, there was left to me nothing from my forty years of building. I could have gone to another land and lived again by my old rules, as Simon, son of John. But I could not come to Jesus as a man of my own making. And I knew there is hope in Christ, and I had to have that hope. I had felt his love, and I could not let it go.

He took me back again, not for what I was worth, but because he loved me. He searched into my deepest heart, so I could know it all. Three times he asked me: "Simon, son of John, do you love me?" Not so that he could know; it was part of my salvation from the hell that I had made, that I should say: "Yes, Lord, I love you."

The church now knows me as he knew me. They know my weakness and they know my cure. What leadership I have today I hold not by my own reason or strength, but in the strength of Jesus' love. And even though the echoes of that laughter in my youth still trouble me, and lead me astray into selfish, prideful acts, my fellow Christians know me and correct me and I am not hurt. For within this church of Jesus there is love, and I need feel no fear of mocking. I know they love me because they love my Lord.

John
A Loving Kindness

Jim Bishop

ohn insisted that he should perform the final loving kindness for his Messiah; Mary could be left with the women. He was ashamed that the other apostles were not present. As the master had warned, they had scattered like sheep when the shepherd was attacked. It grieved John to think that his beloved Jesus might still be in the hands of strangers in these final hours. He said that he would be of service to them; he insisted on it. Who better to lay loving hands on the body than the one to whom he had entrusted his mother?

The little party of women remained near the gate. There was no one else.

The three Marys expressed a desire to send someone into the city to buy rare spices and perfumes. It was the custom for women to do this. The men wanted to agree; but this was going to be a hasty burial, and there was no time. They pointed out that Nicodemus had brought spices, but the women were not impressed. They had offered nothing but tears. They too wanted to be a part of the last loving kindness. John suggested that they could return tomorrow or Sunday with perfumes. He saw the sorrowful disappointment in their faces. Then Joseph of Arimathaea said that the women should supervise the impreg-

nation of the spices in the linen winding cloths. Their heads lifted a little. Joseph was a middle-aged man. He understood women better than the young Apostle.

The men moved on to the cross. . . .

They saw the women approaching. From a distance they could see that Mary of Alpheus and Mary Magdalene were trying to dissuade Jesus' mother, who was pressing forward and weeping. John left the body and hurried to the side of the mother. Softly pleading, he reminded her that Jesus had said that his death was not a defeat, but a glorious victory; that he had come here to perform this act of sacrifice and it would hurt him to know that she mourned. As he argued gently, John too began to weep. . . .

The tomb was not an ornate one. Judged by the standards of those who could afford sepulchers, it was ordinary. It was set in the side of a twelve-foot hill facing the Gate of Gennath and, from front to back, measured fifteen feet. From floor to ceiling, it was seven feet, and from wall to wall about five.

There was an atrium, or open forecourt, in front. The entrance was less than five feet high and was closed by a millstone sixty inches in diameter and nine inches thick. The weight of this stone was beyond the strength of one person to move. It sat in a curved groove and, when two or more men tried to rock it away from the entrance, an extra man had to crouch below with a heavy stone to use as a chock. Whether it was rolled to the left or the right of the entrance, the groove turned upward. The tendency of the stone was always to roll back into place before the aperture.

Behind the stone was a vestibule, about six feet deep and, like the whole, it was hewn from limestone. The ceilings and the walls were roughly finished. A thin ledge of rock separated the vestibule from the main sepulcher. The doorway between was about forty inches high and loved ones always had to bend deeply to enter.

On the right side of the vestibule was a flat slab of stone for the use of visitors who might want to sit. It was on this stone, in cramped quarters, that the three men hurriedly prepared Jesus for final entombment. They lit tapers and stuck them in the walls. Nicodemus was well versed in these matters; and when the body of Jesus had been laid flat, it was he who placed the downy feather under the nose of the deceased

for a specified length of time, which was about fifteen minutes. If, in that time, the feather had not moved, the soul had left the body.

The feather did not move.

THE PLACING IN THE TOMB , Simon Vouet (1590–1649), Musee du Louvre, Paris, France. © Musee du Louvre, Paris/Lauros–Giraudon, Paris/SuperStock (1030-667).

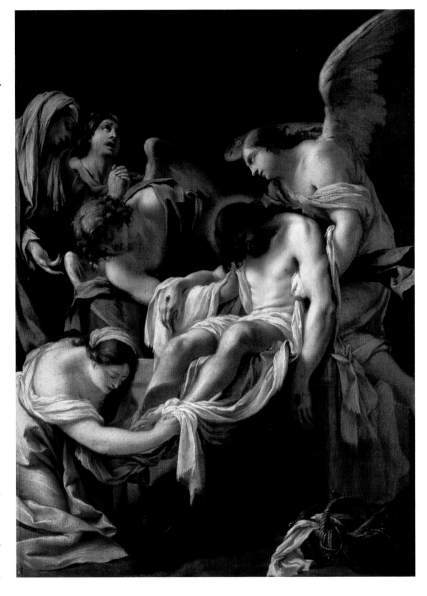

A SHINING TRIUMPH

JIM BISHOP

John hurried out to bring in the three Marys. On the way back, he told them that this was a hasty work, that Jesus was not properly anointed, but, again, that Mary Magdalene and Mary of Alpheus could, on the morrow or on Sunday come with spices and perfumes and pay homage to the Lord.

The interior was dark, except for the fitful shadows and yellow light thrown by the dying tapers. The main part of the sepulcher was so small that the men had to leave in order to allow the women to enter.

They remained a few minutes and, as they stooped to leave, they whispered among themselves that they would be back to do honor to the Messiah. The Magdalene wanted to leave at once to purchase perfumes in the city, but Nicodemus told her that the Sabbath was too close. Besides, the morrow would not be too late.

Nicodemus took the empty spice boxes and the linen strips which were left. He gazed long upon the face of the mother of Jesus. Then, with no farewell, he turned and went away. Joseph bowed to the women, and followed him. Young John looked helplessly at the big millstone, then told Mary, the mother of Jesus, that it was time they started for home. Mary nodded slightly and managed a small smile for her new son. He took her arm, and they left, walking through the garden of wildflowers and up onto the rock shelf where the three uprights stood, and across the roads and through the gate into the Holy City.

It had been a long day, a very long day. There was much to remember, and some would remember it this way and some would remember it that way. Much of it had been done in secret, in spite of the public execution, and it would be weeks before the news reached the small towns of Galilee and the settlements east of Jericho.

The two Marys sat with their backs to the stone. They loved him and, in their love, they missed the enormous triumph; the new promise; the good news.

They did not even notice that the sun was shining.

And when Joseph had taken the body, he wrapped it in a clean linen cloth, And laid it in his own new tomb, which he had hewn out in the rock: and he rolled a great stone to the door of the sepulchre, and departed. And there was Mary Magdalene, and the other Mary, sitting over against the sepulchre (MATTHEW 27:59–61).

The Crypt of Saint John, Akkko, Israel. © R. Opfer/H. Armstrong Roberts (KR–64514).

JOHN

PAM KENNEDY

I am John, a fisherman, the son of a fisher-man, the brother of a fisherman. Years ago I saw before me the life of my father and brother, stretching as wide and clear as the Sea of Galilee. There were nets to mend and boats to repair, fish to be sorted and sold. Life had a texture as comforting and reliable as the pass-ing of seasons.

Then he came. He called, "Follow me" and we could hear no other voices—not the sea, not our friends, not even our father and mother. And so my brother James and I left the nets and followed him, unsure of our motivation, knowing only that we could not resist his call. We would become fishers of men, he said. We didn't know what he meant, but we followed just the same.

He called others, too, until there were twelve of us. Not all were fish-ermen. Some were learned, some were not—we were philosophers, businessmen, tradesmen, rebels. But we were all seekers and we fol-lowed him, looking for answers even before we had fully formed the questions.

For three years we walked and talked and lived with him as he taught us things unfamiliar to our Galilean minds. It was not always easy to understand him; but he was patient like a father working with an eager, but less-than-brilliant child. And we tried to learn and understand because we loved him more than our own lives.

Then he left us. It happened almost before we knew it, although we should have known. The signs were there all along. Always under the surface lurked the hatred, the anger, the scent of murder waiting for its hour. But love never wants to believe in evil, and we refused to see the signs. We talked of faithfulness and greatness in a kingdom yet to come; and he spoke of suffering and crucifixion; and we ignored him. But he knew. He always knew.

When they came, led by the traitor, Judas, to take him away, we scat-tered like frightened chil-dren. Long forgotten were our vows of loyalty. We left our promises in the dark of Gethsemane.

He went freely, although they thought they took him by force. And when he stood before the magis-trates, I hid in shadows and

When Jesus therefore saw his mother, and the disciple standing by, whom he loved, he saith unto his mother, Woman, behold thy son! Then saith he to the disciple, Behold thy mother! And from that hour that disciple took her unto his own home (JOHN 19:26–27).

heard his words. He spoke the truth, yet they didn't understand any more than I had at first. And they hated him because he would not bow before their petty power.

Peter denounced him loudly just as the rooster crowed. But I, in my refusal to speak, denounced him too. Some thought my silence strength, but he and I knew it was not. It was fear as raw and bold as blood.

They marched him to Golgotha, and we few followers clung together in our grief. I watched his mother's face and marveled at its serenity, even as tears streamed down her cheeks. I longed to speak but did not. I wanted to shout my love for him but could not. Somehow, he lifted his poor, anguished head and said, "Here is your mother." I took her home that day after the agony of his death, and wondered at the trust he placed in me, and I was overcome with gratitude.

There was nothing to do, we thought, but gather together and pray. But our prayers seemed as lifeless as his body; and the days continued, broken only by restless sleep.

Then on the morning of the third day, the women came running, gasping with the news of angels and a resurrection. Their words tumbled out in excitement and we determined them hysterical. But something in their eyes gripped my heart. I caught Peter's glance and we ran to the garden tomb.

I arrived there first, but I was paralyzed by awe and fear and could not enter. I stood transfixed, peering in with my hand upon unyielding stone. I saw the strips of linen on the bier, but did not comprehend their import. Then Peter pushed past me roughly. His shout of alarm pulled me forward from my fear, and slowly, tentatively, I entered that place of death.

The morning light streamed in and settled

PETER AND JOHN FOLLOW AFAR OFF, James J. Tissot (1836–1902). © SuperStock (999–9242).

on the empty graveclothes. He was not there! The realization fell on me like the dawning sun. We did not speak; there were no words to clarify our emotions. We ran from the tomb laughing like children, seeing the world afresh, like blind men healed!

In the emptiness of that stony grave, I found fulfillment—not only of my life, but of all the promises he had made. Slowly I began to see the sense of it—the stories, the parables, the prophecies, and the prayers woven together in a tapestry of truth.

And then he came again! He showed himself to us and taught us deeper things we had not understood before. Our grief was gone. The answer to our prayers stood before us, and we walked and talked with him once more. His bright and shining truth drove all doubts out of our minds. Now we could truly fish for men and serve our master well. Denial, failure, abandonment were forgiven once and always.

He departed once more, rising in the morning sky, and we watched him go in glory but were not sad. We will see him again, each in his appointed time. But now we trace the paths before us, that he laid out with love and care. I walk now, hearing only two words: "Follow me."

THE ANGEL OPENS CHRIST'S SEPULCHRE. Oakwood (1612–1652). Szepmuveszeti Muzeum. © Erich Lessing/Art Resource (ART54454).

THE LAST DAYS

GERALD N. BATTLE

He was very old. A bishop of the church who had labored for long in many lands, now confined to his chair and carried daily to the church through the school to greet the children. That was all that was left to him. He was so old his memory played tricks on him. He had dictated for some minutes to his writing clerk when he suddenly remembered that his brother had been dead for more years than he could remember.

Wearily he had shaken his head, dismissed the startled clerk, and asked to be alone. He knew his time was not far off. He welcomed death. Once more he would be reunited with Jesus and the others. Of all the twelve, he was the last. There was one regret. If only he could have merited a glorious death like the others. His brother James had been the first to go—felled by Herod's sword in Jerusalem. Though they had been but twelve—and Paul, of course—they had kept the faith, and the word had spread throughout the world.

Now he alone of that small band was left. There would be no glorious death on the cross for him, no swift blow from an executioner's sword. Only the quiet running out of time for an old man who had tried to understand and teach his understanding to others. He frowned and rapped his cane against the wooden leg of his chair. And then he smiled. He was past ninety, and still the flicker of the old temper remained. There was still a trace of pride that he could not subdue.

Hearing the noise of the cane against the chair, the old man's servant hurried quickly to his side. "Sire, is something wrong?"

"Rouse me early in the morning and take me to the church. It will be for the last time. Early, mind you. Very early. There is not much time left." The old man waved his servant away. He wanted to be alone with his memories.

He tried to make his mind reach back to the early days in Galilee. The distance was too great. He could not make his mind recall. The one thing he remembered best were the words Jesus had taught him long ago: "Love all people, John—all people." He had tried to practice that teaching all his life since Jesus had changed him and his life. The people often smiled affectionately

> For God so loved the world, that he gave his only begotten Son, that whosoever believeth in him should not perish, but have everlasting life (JOHN 3:16).

when he was carried into the church. He would lean down from his chair and touch their heads and say, "Love one another, children, love one another." The people would nod their heads and smile.

Once someone had asked him why he stressed this charge above all others. Smiling to himself now, he recalled his answer. "Love one another. It is enough to remember this. If you do this all the other commandments follow. This is the hardest of them all. Love one another."

Suddenly he was so tired, so tired. He seemed to see a blaze of bright light—a light like he had seen once long ago on Mount Hermon. The cane dropped from his hand. Tomorrow was already here for John.

SAINT JOACHIM, San Gioacchino Vincenzo Foppa (1427–1515). Pinocoteca Civica Castello Sforzesco, Milan, Italy. © SuperStock (457–2180).

And when he had gone a little farther thence, he saw James the son of Zebedee, and John his brother, who also were in the ship mending their nets. And straightway he called them: and they left their father Zebedee in the ship with the hired servants, and went after him. . . . And James the son of Zebedee, and John the brother of James; and he surnamed them Boanerges, which is, The sons of thunder (MARK 1:19–20; 3:17).

JOHN
WILLIAM BARCLAY

John was the son of Zebedee and the brother of James. He was a fisherman by trade, and it was while he and his brother James were engaged in mending their nets in the boat by the lakeside with their father that Jesus called them. . . . . In the first three Gospels, John seldom appears apart from James; for the most part James and John are inseparable, and act and speak as one. From these Gospels there emerges a vivid picture of John—and the strange thing is that it is not an attractive one.

James and John were men of a violent temper. . . . It was no doubt for this reason that John and James received their nickname—*Boanerges*, the sons of thunder, as Jesus called them. They must have been violent and explosive characters, with tempers on a hair trigger and with voices ready to thunder out in denunciation and condemnation. . . .

There is one fragment of tradition which Jerome has handed down to us. "When John tarried in Ephesus to extreme old age, and could only with difficulty be carried to the church in the arms of his disciples, and was unable to give utterance to many words, he used to say no more at their several meetings than this: 'Little children, love one another.' At length the disciples and fathers who were there, wearied with always hearing the same words, said: 'Master, why dost thou always say this?' 'It is the Lord's command,' was his reply, 'and, if this alone be done, it is enough'" (*Commentary of Galatians* 6, 10). In the end John had forgotten everything except his Lord's command of love.

THE ISLAND OF PATMOS, DODECANESE ISLANDS, GREECE. John spent
the last years of his life here. © Superstock (1332-157).

Feed My Sheep

John 21:2–17

There were together Simon Peter, and Thomas called Didymus, and Nathanael of Cana in Galilee, and the sons of Zebedee, and two other of his disciples. Simon Peter saith unto them, I go a-fishing. They say unto him, We also go with thee. They went forth, and entered into a ship immediately; and that night they caught nothing. But when the morning was now come, Jesus stood on the shore: but the disciples knew not that it was Jesus.

Then Jesus saith unto them, Children, have ye any meat?

They answered him, No. And he said unto them, Cast the net on the right side of the ship, and ye shall find.

They cast therefore, and now they were not able to draw it for the multitude of fishes.

Therefore that disciple whom Jesus loved saith unto Peter, It is the Lord.

Now when Simon Peter heard that it was the Lord, he girt his fisher's coat unto him, (for he was naked,) and did cast himself into the sea. And the other disciples came in a little ship; (for they were not far from land, but as it were two hundred cubits,) dragging the net with fishes. As soon then as they were come to land, they saw a fire of coals there, and fish laid thereon, and bread.

Jesus saith unto them, Bring of the fish which ye have now caught.

Simon Peter went up, and drew the net to land full of great fishes, an hundred and fifty and three: and for all there were so many, yet was not the net broken.

Jesus saith unto them, Come and dine. And none of the disciples durst ask him, Who art thou? knowing that it was the Lord.

Jesus then cometh, and taketh bread, and giveth them, and fish likewise. This is now the third time that Jesus showed himself to his disciples, after that he was risen from the dead.

So when they had dined, Jesus saith to Simon Peter, Simon, son of Jonas, lovest thou me more than these?

He saith unto him, Yea, Lord; thou knowest that I love thee.

He saith unto him, Feed my lambs.

He saith to him again the second time, Simon, son of Jonas, lovest thou me?

He saith unto him, Yea, Lord; thou knowest that I love thee.

He saith unto him, Feed my sheep.

He saith unto him the third time, Simon, son of Jonas, lovest thou me?

Peter was grieved because he said unto him the third time, Lovest thou me? And he said unto him, Lord, thou knowest all things; thou knowest that I love thee.

Jesus saith unto him, Feed my sheep.

THE COAST OF THE SEA OF GALILEE, ISRAEL. H. Armstrong Roberts (KR-111941-f).

THE END AND THE BEGINNING

WILLIAM BARCLAY

The cross came as no surprise to Jesus. From the beginning of his life to the end of his life he knew that it was coming. All through his life we can trace his consciousness of the cross. . . .

When he set out for Jerusalem on the last journey, it was "to be received up" (Luke 9:51). Jesus was never in any doubt about what awaited him at the end of the journey. So he set out for Jerusalem, "for it cannot be that a prophet should perish away from Jerusalem" (Luke 13:33). Open-eyed, he took the martyr's road.

And then still another note enters into it. He took the Twelve and told them: "Behold, we are going up to Jerusalem, and everything that is written of the Son of Man by the prophets will be accomplished; for he will be delivered to the Gentiles, and will be mocked and shamefully treated and spit upon; they will scourge him and kill him, and on the third day he will rise" (Luke 19:31–34). The new note is that Jesus was going not to death but to destiny. Here was no sudden emergency situation; it was something in which the will of God was being worked out, and in which the message of the prophets was coming true. "The Son of Man goes as it has been determined" (Luke 22:22). I tell you that this scripture must be fulfilled in me. And he was reckoned with the transgressors; for what is written about me has its fulfillment" (Luke 22:37). Things were not out of control; the will of God was being worked out, that will which in Gethsemane Jesus accepted (Luke 22:42).

What then was Jesus doing in these last days within the shadow of the cross? The prophets of the Old Testament had a special way of getting their message across. It is called dramatic prophetic action. When words had no effect, when people apparently would not listen to or heed words, then the prophet did something, something sensational, vivid and dramatic.

Toward the close of his ministry Jesus repeatedly used dramatic prophetic action. This is what he did when be came riding into Jerusalem at what we call the Triumphal Entry (Luke 19:28–40). In the east the ass was not the despised donkey of the west; the ass was a handsome and noble animal, and it was the animal on which kings rode when they came in peace; they rode on horses only when riding to war. At the Triumphal Entry Jesus made his appeal to men. In dramatic prophetic action more vivid than words he was saying: "Will you take me as your king, not the warrior king, but the king who comes to you in peace?"

When he ate with his men for the last time (Luke 22:14–20), he was saying in dramatic prophetic action: "Look, just as this bread is broken, my body is going to be broken for you. Just as this scarlet wine is poured out, my red lifeblood is going to be poured out—for you." In action more dramatic than words, he was compelling men to look; he was riveting their attention on himself.

And the supreme dramatic action is the cross (Luke 23:24–49). On the cross Jesus was dramatically saying two things. He was saying: "Look! See what sin can do—sin can take the loveliest life that was ever lived and smash it on this cross. Sin is the most destructive thing in all the universe." But he was also saying: "See what love can do. You do this—and I still love you. You crucify me in agony and I pray for your forgiveness. I love you like that!" On the cross there is shown vividly and dramatically the length to which man's sin will go and the length to which God's love will go.

But the cross was not the end. After the cross came the Resurrection, and the Resurrection is the proof that the love of God is not only sacrificial; it is triumphant. It not only suffers; it conquers. It not only dies; it vanquishes death for evermore.

So the risen Christ said two things to his disciples. First, he said to them that all history had been leading up to him (Luke 24:25–27; 44–47). Second, he said that what happened on the cross is designed to make the forgiveness of God available to men. And so, he said, his men must wait until the power of the Holy Spirit came upon them; and then they must go out to preach the suffering and the conquering love of God and to witness to what that love in Jesus Christ had done for them.

We are the descendants of those first disciples. We, too, must look at the cross. We, too, must realize that it was for us he hung and suffered there. Our hearts, too, must be broken in penitence and flooded with forgiveness. We, too, must be clothed with the Holy Spirit. And we, too, in our day and generation must go out to bring the love of God to men and to bring men to the love of God.

CHRIST THE CONSOLER, Carl Heinrich Bloch (1834–1890). © SuperStock (900-100858).

INDEX